# More Praise for
## *South Park Conservatives*

"Brian Anderson's riveting account of the media revolution is a revelation. In a brisk and highly entertaining way, he gives chapter and verse on how the new media is rapidly breaking a liberal stranglehold on both news and entertainment."

—Harry Stein, author of *How I Accidentally Joined the Vast Right-Wing Conspiracy (and Found Inner Peace)*

"Highly entertaining and colorful ... Brian Anderson is one of a limited few writing about the new conservative generation who really 'gets it.' *South Park Conservatives* should be required reading for anyone surprised by the reelection of George W. Bush."

—Lorie Byrd, Polipundit.com

# South Park Conservatives

# South Park Conservatives

The Revolt against Liberal Media Bias

Brian C. Anderson

*Since 1947*
REGNERY
PUBLISHING, INC.
*An Eagle Publishing Company • Washington, DC*

Library of Congress Cataloging-in-Publication Data
Anderson, Brian C., 1961–
  South park conservatives : the revolt against liberal media bias /
Brian C. Anderson.
    p. cm.
  Includes index.
  ISBN 0-89526-019-0
  1.  Mass media—Objectivity—United States. 2.  Conservatism—United
States.  I. Title.
  P96.O242U625 2005
  302.23'0973—dc22
                                    2005001945
Published in the United States by
Regnery Publishing, Inc.
One Massachusetts Avenue, NW
Washington, DC 20001
www.regnery.com

Distributed to the trade by
National Book Network
Lanham, MD 20706

Printed on acid-free paper

Manufactured in the United States of America

10  9  8  7  6  5  4  3  2  1

Books are available in quantity for promotional or premium use. Write to Director of Special Sales, Regnery Publishing, Inc., One Massachusetts Avenue NW, Washington, DC 20001, for information on discounts and terms or call (202) 216-0600.

# Contents

# A New Era

**C**BS's cancellation in late 2003 of its planned four-hour miniseries *The Reagans* marked a watershed in America's culture wars. Ten years earlier, CBS would have happily aired the libelous series—the working script of which depicted, based on zero evidence, the fortieth president declaring himself the Antichrist, dismissing AIDS sufferers with a cruel "They that live in sin shall die in sin," and raging at his staff. Thanks to the remarkable transformation in mass communications and culture that this book chronicles, such left-wing humbug no longer gets a free pass. The consequences for our political life are momentous.

Conservatives have long lamented the Left's near monopoly over the institutions of opinion and information, a monopoly that has enabled liberal opinion-makers to present their views as rock-solid truth and to sweep aside ideas and beliefs they don't like as unworthy of argument. But as CBS discovered to its dismay, the Right now has a sizable media presence of its own. Almost overnight, conservatives have mastered the proliferating new media of talk radio, cable television, and the Internet, and they have benefited from a big shift in book publishing. No longer do the *New York Times*, the big networks, and the rest of the elite liberal media have an all-but-monolithic power to set the terms of the nation's political and cultural debate.

It was Matt Drudge's Internet news site, the Drudge Report, that first leaked script excerpts from *The Reagans* (excerpts that were scheduled to appear in the *New York Times* the next day) and then drove the story. With billions of "hits" a year, the Drudge Report, which shows no bias against the Right, is impossible to ignore. Just ask ultraliberal Barbra Streisand: after Drudge reported that she had spent weeks on *The Reagans* set (where her husband, James Brolin, was portraying the president), she quickly distanced herself from the film. Soon the whole "blogosphere"—the rapidly expanding cybercosmos of commentary and discussion—was buzzing about *The Reagans'* distortions, led by conservative-friendly opinion sites like National Review Online (NRO) and current-event blogs (web diaries) like InstaPundit. Writer Michael Paranzino began a web-based campaign to boycott CBS, and conservative talk radio weighed in. Cable-ratings colossus FOX News, launched in 1996 as a corrective to the media mainstream's left-wing biases, fanned the controversy, booking Paranzino on several shows.

Faced with this new media–driven revolt—unthinkable just a few short years ago—and the subsequent pullout of sponsors, CBS ducked. Network boss Les Moonves shunted *The Reagans* to advertising-free cable subsidiary Showtime, agreeing that the series was unfair to the former president. "It just doesn't work," Moonves told staffers. "Listen, we are not afraid of controversy, we'd go out there if it came in at 50–50, pro and con, but it simply isn't working. It's biased."[1]

In the election year of 2004, the new media turned up the heat. It put CBS right at the center of an even more significant controversy: Rathergate, the liberal media's götterdämmerung. On September 8, CBS News anchor Dan Rather famously took to the air on *60 Minutes II* trumpeting "newly obtained" Texas Air National Guard documents from the early 1970s, which purported to show that President George

W. Bush had neglected his guard duties three decades ago. In a close election, the revelations hurt W.'s reelection hopes—or would have, had they been true.

Rather's "scoop" began to unravel almost instantly, thanks to intrepid bloggers.[2] CBS posted the documents on its website the night of the *60 Minutes II* broadcast. "Buckhead," a conservative lawyer writing in to the conservative FreeRepublic.com site, called the memos forgeries a few hours later, arguing that no machine from the early 1970s could have produced such fonts and spacing. From there, political blogs Power Line (named *Time*'s first annual blog of the year) and Little Green Footballs took over. On the morning of September 9, Power Line's Scott Johnson posted a few paragraphs headed "The 61st Minute," agreeing with Buckhead that the story seemed fishy, and trudged off to his day job as a lawyer. When he got to the office, dozens of reader e-mails were waiting for him, offering evidence as to why the guard documents *had* to be fake. By late morning, Power Line "had an arsenal of arguments attacking the memos—typographical, logical, procedural, historical," as *Time* put it.[3]

Later that afternoon, Little Green Footballs host Charles Johnson, a webpage designer by trade, used Microsoft Word default settings to create a seemingly exact replica of one of the memos. At this point, anyone following the blogosphere sleuthing knew that CBS's story was bogus. These sites had readerships of thousands. But when Drudge linked to Power Line—"60 Minutes Documents on Bush Might Be Fake" blared the headline—millions learned of the rising scandal.

CBS dug in, calling the bloggers "partisan political" operatives. Former CBS News exec and now CNN news head Jonathan Klein, appearing on FOX News, sniffed that the typical blogger was "a guy sitting in his living room in his pajamas writing what he thinks," nothing like CBS's professional news operation, with its "multiple layers of checks and balances." (Klein's comment inspired Jim Geraghty of

NRO's campaign blog the KerrySpot to dub the agents of the blogosphere the "pajamahadeen.") NBC anchor Tom Brokaw accused bloggers of waging a kind of "political jihad against Dan Rather and CBS
News."[4]

But CBS couldn't suppress the truth—not in 2004. A few years ago,
noted InstaPundit's law prof host Glenn Reynolds, "CBS would have
flashed the documents on TV for a few seconds and no one would have
seen them again. Even the people with doubts would have assumed that
CBS had done its legwork." Now the blogosphere—NRO, HughHe-
witt.com, BeldarBlog, RealClearPolitics, RatherBiased.com, and other
sites that had picked up the story—kept fact-checking, reporting the
analyses of experts on typography, National Guard practices, and other
aspects of the controversy. Talk radio started to cover Rathergate "like a
blanket," says veteran radio host Mike Siegel. FOX News did too.[5]

At last, the pressure grew so great that mainstream outlets ABC
News and the *Washington Post* began reporting the story. The *New York
Times* held out a bit longer—it *so* wanted to believe that the story would
hurt Bush that it actually ran a headline proclaiming the memos "Fake
but Accurate." But even the *Times*, which had been embarrassed the
year before by the blogosphere's role in uncovering reporter Jayson
Blair's in-print fabrications, started to snoop around.

What emerged under this new-media and old-media spotlight wasn't
pretty. CBS, it turned out, had received the memos from notorious
Texan Bush-hater Bill Burkett. The network's own document experts
refused to authenticate the memos, and Rather's crew had ignored relevant sources—and anything else that countered the story's anti-Bush
thrust. Worse still, CBS producer Mary Mapes had urged a campaign
aide to Democratic presidential hopeful John Kerry to contact Burkett
about the story—the old media conspiring with the Democratic Party
to bring down a Republican president. It was a paradigmatic case of
liberal media bias—mendacity, even.

Anchorman Rather grudgingly admitted the memos were suspect on September 20. CBS News, its reputation shredded, appointed a two-member investigative team to determine how the unreliable story had made it onto the air. Rather announced he would step down as anchor in March 2005. The investigative panel's 234-page report—decried by some critics as a whitewash, since it refused to acknowledge the role liberal bias at the network played in the scandal and left unanswered several key questions about sources—resulted in CBS's firing of four senior executives, including Mapes.

A third example of the new media's power: the Swift Boat Veterans for Truth story, a key reason John Kerry wasn't taking the oath of office on January 20, 2005. Kerry's advisers later admitted that they should have responded to the Swiftees' charges about the senator's Vietnam record—among them, that he had obtained most of his medals under dubious circumstances, that he had lied about a purported illegal mission to Cambodia in 1968, and that when he returned stateside and testified that he had witnessed war crimes committed by American troops (and indeed joined in them), he had "grossly and knowingly distorted the conduct" of his fellow servicemen, giving aid and comfort to the enemy. But as journalist and historian Michael Barone explains, the Kerry camp didn't respond, "because they were confident the old media would bury the story."

And they were right about that much. The Swiftees couldn't get any old-media traction, even after the book *Unfit for Command*, written by a Swift Boat veteran, appeared in the summer and searing anti-Kerry ads began to run. "The old media loved the Kerry narrative—decorated hero returns from Vietnam and opposes the war—and didn't want to disturb it by airing the Swiftees' charges," says Barone.

The new media again made all the difference. Talk radio, the blogs, and FOX News put the Swiftees' case before the public, blasting *Unfit for Command* to the top of the bestseller list. Kerry weakly and belatedly responded in late August, forcing the old media to pay attention at last. Most of the mainstream coverage was dismissive, but by then some of the charges—which Kerry never succeeded in rebutting—had stuck. "Memo to future Democratic nominees," advises Barone: "You can no longer rely on the old media to hush up stories that hurt your cause. Your friends in the old media don't have a monopoly any more."[6] Fittingly, aging liberal grandee Bill Moyers devoted his final PBS program to "the biggest story of our time": the arrival of conservatives in media. To him, this represented a threat to America, since only liberals should get to decide and disseminate what is newsworthy.

In the chapters ahead, I will demonstrate this paradigm shift and explain its repercussions. We'll look at the old media regime and the invective-filled but flaccid style of argument it permitted the Left to peddle for so long—an illiberal liberalism that has grown even more hysterical as the new media have rendered it less effectual. We will then consider the various agents of change: talk radio, cable TV (above all FOX News), the blogosphere, and book publishing.

There's another dimension to the transformation, less immediately political than cultural: The new media have nourished a fiercely anti-liberal comedic spirit, whose anarchic, vulgar archetype is Comedy Central's brilliant cartoon series *South Park*, depicting the adventures of four foulmouthed fourth-graders. As we'll see, this spirit leaves no politically correct idol standing. *South Park* has mocked—with scathing genius—hate-crime laws and sexual harassment policies, liberal celebrities, abortion-rights extremists, and other shibboleths of the Left.

This anti-Left ethos is particularly appealing to the young, however much it might offend older conservatives. "If people wonder why anti-war celebrities such as Janeane Garofalo or Michael Moore failed to win over the younger generation, you have only to watch *South Park* to see why," says blogger Andrew Sullivan, who coined the phrase "South

Park Republicans" to describe partisans of this iconoclastic attitude (Tech Central Station contributor Stephen Stanton has further popularized the term). "The next generation sees through the cant and piety, and cannot help giggling."[7] By no means, however, has the Right conquered popular culture; television entertainment, especially on the networks, remains mostly liberal in sensibility, and everyone knows where Hollywood stands politically. But it's no longer a liberal monopoly: A new post-liberal counterculture has emerged.

Finally, we'll meet some young conservatives, some of whom you'd call South Park conservatives. The same forces that are reshaping the information landscape are beginning to influence campus life too—the last place, after the media, that conservatives believed the Left's power would remain inviolate. The change isn't coming from faculty or school officials, but from self-organizing students and innovative outside groups, who are taking advantage of the new media to open schools to conservative currents of thought.

So is *South Park Conservatives* the triumphant (or, if you're a lefty, disastrous) story of conservatives winning the culture wars? In my conclusion, I'll argue that such an inference would be too hasty. But it *is* unquestionably time to say that the Right is no longer losing.

# Chapter One

# The Old Media Regime

In his recent book *Weapons of Mass Distortion*, L. Brent Bozell III, head of the Media Research Center (MRC), a media watchdog group, recounts a "rare glimpse behind the curtain" during a CNN appearance that captures the visceral dislike of conservatism—and conservatives—prevalent in the mainstream media. CNN had invited Bozell to debate a new MRC study showing how poorly the news networks covered religion. The CNN panel, to Bozell's delight, proved both civil and fair, "the rare cable television appearance where the discussion did not devolve into a fight," he notes.

In the CNN control room, however, such respect was sorely lacking. CNN had forgotten to turn off the transmission in Bozell's earpiece, so he could hear everything the producers and other staffers were saying—even screaming—as he spoke on air. "Every time I made a statement it was met with derisive insults—*'Goddamn Nazi!' 'Fucking fascist!' 'What an asshole you are!'*—and hysterical laughter," Bozell recalls.

After the program, Bozell bumped into one of the producers standing outside the control room. "Great show," the producer said, beaming. "I couldn't resist," Bozell says. "I reached past him and swung open the control room door. There, crunched in the tight quarters, were a good half dozen CNN employees chattering away. . . . Smiling, I tossed them the earpiece. 'Next time, don't forget to turn it off during the show' was all I needed to say: The picture of this motley crew, big-eyed, their mouths hanging open, will be with me forever."[1]

::          ::          ::

A few years ago, CBS anchor Dan Rather called liberal press bias "one of the great political myths." "Most reporters don't know whether they're Republican or Democrat, and vote every which way," said Rather. His ABC counterpart Peter Jennings agreed. "ABC, CBS, NBC are mainstream media," he reassured CNN's Larry King. "We are largely in the center, without particular axes to grind."[2]

What a load of hooey. Long before Rathergate, long before ex–CBS newsman Bernard Goldberg's bestseller *Bias: A CBS Insider Exposes How the Media Distort the News*, it was clear to any sensible observer that the mass communications media that emerged as powerful opinion-shaping forces after World War II—the national dailies, the Big Three networks, the shiny newsweeklies—were completely dominated by liberals. "If you talk to journalists who cover Washington," FOX News anchor and former ABC News reporter Brit Hume recently noted, "you won't find many who are pro-life, you won't find very many who are environment-movement skeptics, you won't find very many who think that the NRA's anything other than a menace. You will find very few who are Republicans, and you won't find very many who are self-acknowledged conservatives. It's just not there."[3]

Studies galore over the last few decades reinforce Hume's observation. Contrary to Rather's contentions, liberals vastly outnumber conservatives in elite press ranks. Social scientists S. Robert Lichter and Stanley Rothman first documented the imbalance in a pioneering 1979–1980 study later developed into a major book, *The Media Elite*.

Surveying 240 leading journalists at the nation's prestigious media outlets—including the *New York Times*, the *Washington Post*, *Time*, *Newsweek*, ABC, CBS, NBC, and PBS—Lichter and Rothman discovered that eight out of ten voted Democratic in presidential races between 1964 and 1976, with 94 percent picking LBJ over Barry Goldwater in 1964 and 81 percent choosing McGovern over Nixon (who, recall, won 61 percent of the popular vote). The majority of these Watergate-era journalists—54 percent—placed themselves squarely on the left, the authors found. Only 19 percent said they were right of center.[4]

In their economic and social policy views, the authors showed, these journalists tended to be European-style social democrats, if not out-and-out socialists. Two-thirds, for instance, believed that government should significantly shrink the income gap between rich and poor, and an even greater majority endorsed racial preferences for blacks. Culturally, the media elites overwhelmingly embraced 1960s do-your-own-thing values. Nine out of ten gave a thumbs-up to abortion rights, and more than half saw nothing wrong with adultery. Most were not religious. On the foreign policy front, a majority of journalists—Vietnam-haunted—viewed the United States as an exploiter of the Third World, a cause of global poverty, and an immoral squanderer of the world's resources. We were the bad guys, as bad as the Communists we were fighting, maybe worse. The media elites, in short, belonged to what critic Lionel Trilling famously called "the adversary culture," expressing an "actually subversive intention" toward traditional American politics, society, and values.[5]

Nor have things changed since Lichter and Rothman did their original survey. Research from the mid-1990s, conducted by Rothman and political scientist Amy E. Black and written up in *The Public Interest* in 2001, revealed that 76 percent of top journalists voted for Democratic loser Michael Dukakis in the 1988 presidential race, and 91 percent pulled the lever for Bill Clinton in 1992. More than 70 percent felt that the government should guarantee jobs, and 97 percent supported abortion rights. Three-quarters of journalists thought homosexuality was just as acceptable as heterosexuality.[6] You'd have a hard time finding a more liberal group of Americans outside university faculty lounges. And the nation's elite pressrooms seem to be becoming more liberal still, if that's possible. According to a 2004 Pew Research Center survey, only 7 percent of reporters at national news organizations now say that they're conservative; five times that percentage call themselves liberals. *New York Times* reporter John Tierney, one of that paper's few non-lefty writers, surveyed 153 journalists at the 2004 Democratic National Convention. The Washington press corps rooted for Kerry over Bush by a margin of twelve to one, Tierney found, with the outside-the-Beltway reporters endorsing the Massachusetts senator for president by a three-to-one margin.

In virtually every respect, the political and moral views that dominate the media elite have been and remain out of sync with those of the American people. A 2001 Gallup poll found that 41 percent of Americans identify themselves as conservatives; just 18 percent say that they're liberal. More than 40 percent of Americans embrace a pro-life stance on abortion, and a majority thinks that abortion is too easy to obtain. Same-sex marriage is a nonstarter. Only 4 percent of U.S. citizens endorse tax hikes. Most Americans reject affirmative action. Support for the military runs high.

::        ::        ::

"Wait a second," say some pressmen, when confronted with such facts. "Maybe we journalists are usually liberals, but that doesn't mean we allow our political views ever to influence our reporting. We're pros."

That'd be great, if it were true. But editors and journalists must *choose* what is newsworthy, which experts to consult and how to identify them, what images to run with text or voice-overs, and what questions to raise. Whether intentionally or unconsciously, the press corps's liberal values invariably influence those choices, as the evidence shows.

Consider—to take only one of countless examples of liberal bias collected by the Media Research Center since its founding in 1987—how the Big Three networks reported Bush's proposed tax-reduction package when debate raged over it in early 2001. In ninety-three stories, the MRC points out, the networks quoted liberal critics who disparaged the tax cut as "massive" or "huge" five times more frequently than they quoted tax-cut backers arguing the opposite point. Network reporters, with anchors Dan Rather (CBS) and Tom Brokaw (NBC) taking the lead, called the cuts "big" or "very big" thirty different times; no reporter ever branded the Bush cuts as moderate or small, as some supply-side economists did. Media message: Stop those crazy tax cutters!

The press simply doesn't give the Right a fair shake on the economy. In an important econometric study, American Enterprise Institute researchers Kevin Hassett and John Lott methodically surveyed headlines in hundreds of newspapers and AP reports on unemployment, GDP, retail sales, and durable-goods orders going back to 1985, and found them to be considerably gloomier overall when a Republican sat in the White House, regardless of the economic data the stories reported. For the same kind of economic news, Republican presidents received about 20 to 30 percent less positive coverage from all papers, and 20 to 40 percent less positive coverage from the nation's ten leading papers. Among the most biased news sources were—no surprises here—the *New York Times* and the *Washington Post*. This "partisan gap," as Hassett and Lott call it, distorts public perceptions of the economy. Positive headlines actually had more to do with whether people thought an economy was getting better than with the underlying economic data, the authors unsurprisingly discovered.[7]

Throughout 2004, economists wondered why the public remained grumpy about the Bush economy, whose growth rate matched any twelve-month period of the Clinton presidency. A July AP/Ipsos–Public Affairs survey, for example, found that 57 percent of the respondents thought that the economy had lost more jobs than it had gained over the previous six months, when in fact it had added more than one million jobs. Headlines like the *Chicago Tribune*'s, greeting news of robust 4 percent economic growth during the fourth quarter of 2003—"GDP Growth Disappoints: Job Worries Linger"—no doubt had something to do with the public mystification.

Then there's the way the mainstream media covers the homeless. During the Reagan years, Bernard Goldberg wryly observes, "I started noticing that the homeless people we showed on the news didn't look very much like the homeless people I was tripping over on the sidewalk."[8] In fact, the typical Reagan-era TV-news homeless person looked like your hard-working family-man neighbor, suddenly, catastrophically down on his luck because of a bad economy and a lack of "affordable housing," not the drug-addled, gibberish-spouting, fist-waving deinstitutionalized lunatic he was likely to be in the real world. "The networks insistently editorialized that homelessness was something that could happen to anybody, black or white, rich or poor, and was a consequence of Ronald Reagan's lack of support for federal housing programs," explains *Forbes*'s Dan Seligman; the homeless people shown on the tube had to reinforce that it's-all-Reagan's-fault message.[9] When Democrat Bill Clinton became president, many observers commented, the homeless (of all kinds) curiously vanished from the nightly news and the morning paper headlines, only to return in 2000 when Republican George W. Bush took office.

The old media regime's liberal distortions also color the reporting on cultural controversies like abortion. As the MRC documents, elite reporters rarely label abortion supporters as "liberal" but often tag abortion foes as "conservative"—and never "pro-life." Pro-life protests win little or no coverage, regardless of their size. Worse still, significant new data that show the anti-abortion side gaining ground also go virtually unreported. The Center for the Advancement of Women's stunning 2003 survey showed that 51 percent of women now do not support abortion at all or only in the cases of incest or rape. This drew nary a comment from the Big Three, the *New York Times*, or the *Washington Post*. "We simply don't get the truth on the abortion issue from the liberal media," says Brent Bozell.[10]

::     ::     ::

Liberal bias is perhaps at its most egregious in war reporting, at least when a Republican is president doing the warring. During the Cold War, especially after Ronald Reagan became president, American journalists, like most Western journalists, frequently gave the propaganda of the Soviet Union and its satellites equal footing with American officials' statements, a Media Institute study documented. On CBS's *This Morning* in 1988, hostess Kathleen Sullivan was sadly representative of this tendency, thrilling over Fidel Castro's police state: "Now half of the Cuban population is under the age of twenty-five, mostly Spanish-speaking, and all have benefited from Castro's Cuba, where their health and their education are priorities."

The great anti-Communist writer Jean-François Revel denounced such naiveté in his mammoth study of elite political folly, *The Flight from Truth*. "A great deal of 'reporting' then done by Western journalists was primarily aimed at justifying the existence of [totalitarian] systems and soft-pedaling the threat they posed to democracy in various parts of the world," wrote Revel. "This was a classic example of how democracy can unwittingly transmute its lifeblood into a poison, by fabricating arguments to prove that, unless absolutely perfect, it does not deserve to exist. In effect, this amounted to stipulating that democracy's only choice is between saintliness and death."[11]

When wars become hot, the writer and critic Dinesh D'Souza notes, the enduring "meta story"—the hidden general premise that governs elite press and broadcast coverage—is "another Vietnam." "Every time the United States intervenes abroad," complains D'Souza, whether in Grenada or Bosnia or Afghanistan or now Iraq, "a chorus of voices in the media warns that it's Vietnam all over again." "Quagmire," "bogged-down," "grim"—the elite press rushes to depict U.S. military action in the harshest light possible; civilian casualties get played up, heroic soldiers played down. It doesn't matter how often the story turns out wrong, says D'Souza. "It is embedded in the psyche of a media generation that came of age during the Vietnam era."[12]

The defeatist coverage of the Afghanistan and Iraq wars illustrates the meta story's continuing hold on many journalists and editors. Just four weeks into the United States's successful drive to remove the Taliban from power in Afghanistan in the fall of 2001, for example, the *New York Times*'s R. W. Apple saw only calamity ahead. "The ominous word 'quagmire' has begun to haunt conversations among government officials and students of foreign policy," he wrote.[13] Mere days later, the Taliban regime fell. ABC News, to take another case, lent undue credence to Taliban claims of Afghan civilian casualties, running sixteen minutes' worth of reports on them from October 8–31. Those claims proved wildly exaggerated.

Reporting on Iraq has been bleaker still. Even as General Tommy Franks was leading American forces to swift victory in direct military conflict in spring 2003, the elite press proclaimed imminent U.S. defeat, trumpeted every purported injustice or error committed by our troops, and, Cold War–style, even sympathized with the enemy. "Iraqis Show New Defiance"; "Baghdad Bombing Brings Back Memories of 9/11"; "Urban Warfare: Long a Key Part of an Underdog's Down-to-Earth Arsenal" (on the Iraqi forces' practice of hiding behind civilians)—these were typical headlines in the elite press. In the hard struggle to pacify and reconstruct Iraq, where the United States has admittedly taken some questionable steps, old-media reporters, with a few notable exceptions (above all, the *New York Times*'s sterling John Burns), have ignored progress and highlighted every impediment to victory. It's as if they want the Iraq War to fail.[14]

Along with the gloomy reporting on military affairs comes an indulgent—even celebratory—view of antiwar types. "It's an extraordinarily diverse crowd," CNN reporter Maria Hinojosa gushed in a representative early 2003 television segment about a throng of protesters opposing then-looming military intervention in Iraq. "I have seen elderly men and women with mink coats carrying their posters. I have also seen children with their parents coming from public schools. . . . I have seen old antiwar folks who say that they've been coming to demonstrations since the 1960s, as well as high school students and college students who have never taken part in any demonstration who are now becoming part of the activity here."

If you hadn't come across the polls showing strong support for taking out Saddam at the time, you might think *all* Americans stood firmly against war. In thirty-eight different stories on antiwar street demonstrations, CNN noted only once that most Americans did not support the protesters' views. One thing was certain: CNN, like its mainstream media brethren, sure did.

The elite media's antiwar stance—sometimes coming close to an outright anti-Americanism—has been a major factor in driving viewers and readers away from it and toward FOX News, the blogosphere, and other news alternatives, as we'll come to later.

::    ::    ::

Far from keeping its liberal sympathies in check, the elite press sometimes roots for the Dems so openly it's laughable. Never was this truer than in the 2004 election campaign. It was as if the rise of alternative media, giving the Right a real chance to gets its word out in public debate for the first time, also gave some in the mainstream media the excuse to drop even the pretense of objectivity, so as to lobby night and day for the Democratic ticket. Rathergate and the Swift Boat vets controversy were only the most prominent cases. But the old media's traditional bias found itself, for the first time, nakedly exposed in the light cast by the new information sources.

"Long a Republican Bulwark, a Growing Arizona Is in Play," blared a front-page *Los Angeles Times* headline on the presidential race in September 2004. You had to read through most of the article before discovering that polls then had Bush eclipsing Kerry by sixteen points in Arizona. Bush eventually won the state handily.

Or how about the late-September Associated Press hit job camouflaged as a news story, headlined "Bush Twists Kerry's Words on Iraq," which could easily have been written by the Kerry campaign? Oh, wait, maybe it was. As the Power Line blog reminded everybody, the AP campaign reporter who wrote the story, Jennifer Loven, is married to Kerry environmental adviser Roger Ballentine and had dumped on President Bush before. Indeed, in an earlier "news" piece on the Bush administration's Clear Skies environmental initiative, Loven dubbed it the "so-called" Clear Skies legislation, and criticized it in language lifted directly from one of her husband's policy articles. Power Line's John Hinderaker seethed, "If Jennifer Loven wants to run around and be a spokesperson for her Kerry-contributing and Kerry-paid husband's environmental views, she should be free to do so, JUST NOT AS A FREAKING AP REPORTER FOR THE PRESIDENTIAL CAMPAIGN."[15]

After John Kerry emerged as the Democratic nominee, the elite media followed Democratic chairman Terry McAuliffe "like Pavlov's dogs," says media critic Tim Graham. "McAuliffe rang the 'AWOL' bell on President Bush's service in the Texas Air National Guard, and the

networks followed, with sixty-three morning- and evening-news seg-
ments on the Big Three networks pounding Bush to prove he wasn't
'AWOL,'" Graham points out.[16] In 1992, the networks aired only ten
evening news stories on Bill Clinton's draft evasion after that story
broke. Kerry's Vietnam record—Kerry's record in general—remained
largely unexamined by mainstream media outlets during the 2004 race.

Even more damning was the October memo from ABC News's
respected political director, Mark Halperin, which was leaked to the
blogosphere. It basically instructed his colleagues to be tougher on
Bush than on Kerry. "Kerry distorts, takes out of context, and [makes]
mistakes all the time," Halperin averred, but these untruths are "not
central to his efforts to win." By contrast, Bush's attacks on Kerry
"involve distortions and taking things out of context in a way that goes
beyond what Kerry has done." An implausible claim, but never mind:
"We have a responsibility to hold both sides accountable to the public
interest, but that doesn't mean we reflexively and artificially hold both
sides 'equally' accountable when the facts don't warrant that," Halperin
told his troops, adding obligingly, "It's up to Kerry to defend himself, of
course."[17] But ABC could help!

Conservatives were justifiably ornery over the memo. "Halperin
should make it official and move down to Washington to join the
Democratic National Committee," radio host Laura Ingraham sarcastically commented, expressing widespread sentiment.[18] Yet, as *New
York Post* columnist John Podhoretz advised, the memo was uniquely
useful evidence, revealing "as no other document ever has the existence
of a deeply ingrained double standard in the way political news is
reported in the United States."[19] The elite media predictably looked
away from Halperin's blatant side-taking, though it had gotten all
worked up a few months earlier over ostensibly pro-Bush programming
notes from Halperin's FOX News counterpart John Moody (we'll consider those in Chapter Four).

Not that ABC could come close to the *New York Times*'s Bush-bashing, which encompassed far more than its innumerable pessimistic stories on Iraq—including its front-page report, broken just days before the presidential election and swiftly debunked by NBC and legions of bloggers, about 380 tons of high explosives purportedly missing from Iraq's Al Qaqaa military complex south of Baghdad. The *Times* did everything in its power to bring down W., from burying good news for the president deep in polling articles to magnifying and promoting the charges of administration critics like Richard Clarke and Joseph Wilson to coming up with the absurd "Fake but Accurate" headline.

At the Unity convention for minority journalists in summer 2004, many attendees snickered during President Bush's address but interrupted candidate Kerry's address with enthusiastic cheers and whistles. One reporter present found the display of partisanship galling. "It was so offensive and awful, and I hated it. It was clearly inappropriate." Another felt the same way: "As a group we should have kept ourselves in check."[20]

Do we really need further proof of the mainstream media's transparent politicking in the 2004 presidential race? Well, here's just a little more. S. Robert Lichter's nonpartisan Center for Media and Public Affairs studied 2004 election coverage by the Big Three, *Time*, and *Newsweek* during the summer and found evaluations of John Kerry ran 67 percent positive. For W., they ran 60 percent negative. Kerry enjoyed "the best press on network news of any presidential nominee since we began tracking election news in 1988," the Center said. *Newsweek* reporter Evan Thomas, who said "absolutely" that most reporters wanted to see Kerry in the White House, estimated that the bias perhaps bought an extra five points at the polls for the Dems—not enough to win, as it turned out.[21]

Bush's reelection came as a big shock to some in the old media, like CBS *MarketWatch* commentator Jon Friedman, who deserves the 2004

Pauline Kael Award for liberal cocooning. (Following Richard Nixon's landslide victory in the 1972 presidential race, Kael famously snapped, "I don't know how Richard Nixon could have won. I don't know anybody who voted for him.") "The Bush political team intuitively understood the tone of the U.S. voters much better than the media did," Friedman reflected after the 2004 election. "To be honest, I still don't quite understand how certified media junkies like me could have been so wrong. I read the *New York Times* and *The New Yorker* religiously. I watch CNN and the networks' evening news programs as well as the gabfests on Sunday mornings too. Go figure."[22]

Go figure indeed. Thanks to the revolutionary changes in mass communications this book explores—changes that have helped expose the elite media's biases—and partly because Americans have got eyes to see, many have come to distrust the leading news organizations, believing they skew the news left. (Friedman might be joining their ranks soon.) In a 2003 Gallup poll, for instance, 45 percent of adult Americans described the media as "too liberal," compared with just 15 percent who saw it as "too conservative." The Pew Research Center found much the same in a 2003 survey: 51 percent of respondents felt the press had a left-wing bias, while 26 believed it tilted right. After Rathergate, a nationwide Gallup poll found only 44 percent of Americans were confident of the media's ability to report the news fairly and accurately. That was the lowest percentage that Gallup had recorded since it began canvassing Americans on the subject over thirty years ago.

::      ::      ::

Reinforcing the liberalism of the press, as everyone knows, is the liberalism of network entertainment—"the America Dream machine," as Lichter, his wife, Linda S. Lichter, and Rothman call it in their 1994 book *Prime Time: How TV Portrays American Culture*, another groundbreaking study on media and politics. Logging thousands of hours studying the content of prime-time situation comedies and dramas, the authors charted the dramatic shift from the apolitical programming of the 1950s to the "socially relevant" *All in the Family*s and *Maude*s of the 1970s and beyond, in which liberal values became omnipresent, as they largely remain on network entertainment today.

Among their findings:

> In the post-1970s Hollywood imagination, businessmen became villains, in keeping with the fashionable anti-capitalism of Hollywood's millionaire elites. Only 37 percent of the fictional entrepreneurs played positive roles, and the proportion of "bad guy businessmen" was almost double that of all other occupations. What's more, they were *really* nasty, committing 40 percent of the murders and 44 percent of the vice crimes. "The typical exploits of a television business bad guy make the worst robber baron seem a candidate for canonization," Lichter, Lichter, and Rothman wrote. By contrast, lawyers, teachers, social workers, and others who worked in liberal professions benefited from mostly sunny portrayals.

> Only 8 percent of prime-time criminals were black, the authors also pointed out, even though blacks accounted for more than one-third of all Americans arrested for serious crimes, and a majority of those arrested for murders. Black crime that did make it to the small screen tended to be explained away as an understandable reaction to a racist, unjust society. The big network entertainment divisions were as politically correct about race as were any institutions in America.

> Leaving the separate spousal beds and family values of 1950s TV behind, network entertainment embraced the sexual revolution with gusto. Unmarried sex (including by teens), adultery, homosexuality, having kids out of wedlock—all became prime-

time normalcy, with negative portrayals of such behavior vanishingly rare. Characters embodying traditional values, by contrast, became repressed, even malevolent, scolds.[23]

The dream machine's countercultural values are no more surprising than the mainstream news media's liberal biases, once you take into account the beliefs of the "cream of television's creative community." Polling 104 leading writers, producers, and executives, Lichter, Lichter, and Rothman showed that around 75 percent placed themselves on the left, 82 percent voted for George McGovern, and 93 percent said they rarely, if ever, attended religious services—in each case, showing themselves to be dramatically at odds with the American people as a whole.

In 2003, CNN and *Washington Post* media critic Howard Kurtz asked *West Wing* screenwriter and political analyst Lawrence O'Donnell why network dramas never feature any credible Republican characters. "One thing these programs have in common, conservatives are practically invisible," Kurtz said. "President Bartlett in *The West Wing* is a Democrat. Martin Sheen, in fact, made antiwar ads before the invasion of Iraq. 'Mr. Sterling' is a California liberal based loosely on Jerry Brown. Why aren't there any Republicans?" O'Donnell replied with commendable honesty: "You will never get that TV show. You'll never, ever get the Republican TV show. The Writers Guild of America, my union, is at a minimum, 99 percent leftist liberal and, like me, socialist. And we don't know how to write it. We don't."[24]

::     ::     ::

This liberal media universe *was* the mass media until quite recently. A few well-known conservatives (William F. Buckley, George Will, Robert Novak) worked within that universe, but they were lonely figures. To the extent radio broadcasters covered news, they tended to mirror the liberal values of the rest of the press. Nor were New York's major publishing houses more hospitable to the Right than CBS News or *Newsweek*; if a conservative wanted to get his book published, he had precious few options, as we'll see in Chapter Seven.

The Right had some influential publications—*HUMAN EVENTS*, the flagship *National Review* (from 1955), and Russell Kirk's *The Modern Age*, of course, and a bit later, highbrow neoconservative journals like *Commentary* and *The Public Interest*, and by the time the 1990s got rolling, a rich universe of magazines (*The New Criterion*, *First Things*, *City Journal*, *The Weekly Standard*)—and it had the *Wall Street Journal*'s influential op-ed page and a few other smaller outlets. Yet sum it all up and liberals outgunned the Right in the mediasphere by, I don't know...let's say a ten-to-one advantage, probably a lot more. Add the campuses and big philanthropies, almost completely controlled by the Left, and things looked even worse for conservatives, though by the 1980s the first-rate work of right-of-center think tanks like the American Enterprise Institute began to make a difference in the production of research.

The old-media regime long made it hard for the Right to get a fair hearing for its ideas and beliefs. But before we get to the exciting story of how the new media are overthrowing this old regime, we need to understand one of its most pernicious effects: the way it has nourished an illiberal spirit on the Left.

# Chapter Two

# Illiberal Liberalism

"Racist," "homophobe," "sexist," "mean-spirited," "insensitive"—it has become an ugly habit of left-liberal political argument to dismiss conservative ideas as if they don't deserve a hearing, and to redefine mainstream conservative views as extremism and bigotry. A sympathetic old-media regime has allowed liberals to get away with this tendency to argue by invective, rather than to debate ideas seriously, and it has sheltered them from recognizing just how shopworn their ideas have become. The rise of the new Right-friendly media I will analyze in the chapters ahead has made this illiberal, politically correct tendency even more hysterical and strident, since it is forcing liberals to defend their positions, something many have little experience with, resent deeply, and—often enough—do poorly. It has also rendered the demagoguery far less effective: The truth can now get out.

And that's no inconsequential thing. Illiberal liberalism undermines two principles crucial to liberal democracy and central to its superiority to other forms of government.

First, democracy requires a willingness to engage the arguments of those you disagree with, recognizing their equality as citizens. Sure, this noble ideal inevitably takes its lumps in the bruised-knuckle world of real politics; as Frederick Douglass once pointed out, those who look for politics to be unfailingly polite "want rain without thunder and lightning."[1] But calling someone a racist or a bigot says that his ideas have no place in the democratic public square. It's an annihilating gesture, appropriately directed against an Islamofascist out to destroy America and not against the principled beliefs of your conservative fellow citizen.

The second ingredient of liberal democracy that elite-media–nourished illiberalism denies is a belief in the superiority of argument over force. The very first paragraph of the *Federalist Papers* made reason central to the American political project: "[I]t seems to have been reserved to the people of this country, by their conduct and example," wrote Alexander Hamilton, "to decide the important question, whether societies of men are really capable or not of establishing good government from *reflection* and *choice*, or whether they are forever destined to depend for their political constitutions on accident and force."[2] Without reflection—reason—politics degenerates into tyranny. The founders understood this.

::      ::      ::

In public discussion during the now-ending era of mainstream media domination, liberals haven't engaged in much reasoned argument with conservatives. Consider, as paradigmatic, how liberals—including even some ostensibly centrist Democratic politicians—have conducted themselves in the debate over affirmative action. Conservatives argue that racial hiring or admission preferences for blacks contravene the basic American ideal that all people should be treated equally under the law—the ideal that inspired the original civil rights movement. Moreover, these preferences penalize non-blacks who have committed no wrong, conservatives say, and they end up harming blacks by demoralizing and stigmatizing them as somehow in need of special help to get ahead. You might disagree with these ideas, but they're principled, coherent, and democratic. Yet liberals have long gotten away with dismissing them, and those who hold them, as racist.

Several years ago, for example, the then vice president Al Gore gave a speech to an NAACP convention that perfectly embodies the typical liberal response to criticism of racial preferences. "I've heard the critics of affirmative action," Gore said. "They use their 'color blind' the way duck hunters use a duck blind—they hide behind it and hope the ducks won't notice." *Boston Globe* columnist Jeff Jacoby incredulously responded, "Hunters use a duck blind to kill ducks. What can Gore be saying? That affirmative action's critics want to kill—blacks?"[3] Apparently so, for Gore went on in the speech to demand to know the reaction of racial-preference opponents to a horrendous crime in Virginia, in which a black man "was doused with gasoline, burned alive, and decapitated by two men."

Not a week goes by without a prominent liberal stooping to this tactic. "[Liberals'] efforts to . . . stereotype their adversaries as racists have become so routine as to seem unremarkable," laments the *National Journal*'s Stuart Taylor, Jr.[4]

Out of hundreds of examples, a few will have to suffice. Speaking in September 2004 to the National Baptist Convention, the nation's largest black church group, Democratic standard-bearer John Kerry thundered, "The wrong choices of the Bush administration— reduced taxes for the few and reduced opportunities for the middle class and those struggling to join it—are taking us back to two Americas, separate and unequal. . . . Our cities and communities are being torn apart by forces just as divisive and destructive as Jim Crow."[5] So President Bush, a man who appointed more blacks to senior positions than any previous president and whose education policies are helping to liberate black kids from crummy urban schools, is . . . a neosegregationist? NAACP chairman Julian Bond seemed to think so too. He denounced the president for being in thrall to a party whose "idea of equal rights is the American flag and Confederate swastika flying side by side."[6]

But Kerry, who also made the contemptible accusation that Bush suppressed a million black votes to win in 2000, was just following the Clinton-Gore playbook. President Clinton compared the promoters of the California Civil Rights Initiative—the ultimately successful 1996 ballot measure banning discrimination based on race or sex in state programs—with, you guessed it, segregationists. Christopher Edley, a Harvard law professor who served as President Clinton's key adviser on race, referred to Abigail and Stephan Thernstrom's measured 1997 book, *America in Black and White*, as a "crime against humanity" for its anti-preferences stance.[7]

::          ::          ::

The illiberal liberals discover racism not just behind opposition to racial preferences but behind most conservative ideas and policy recommendations. When the Newt Gingrich–led Republicans wanted to cut taxes in the mid-1990s, Harlem's Democratic congressman Charles Rangel charged race hatred: "It's not 'spic' or 'nigger' anymore," Rangel growled. "They say, 'Let's cut taxes.'"[8] Speaking on ABC's *This Week*, feminist and Al Gore consultant Naomi Wolf causally accused George W. Bush's advisers—by whom she meant *City Journal* editor Myron Magnet—of being "racist." Wolf's evidence? The truthful observation that some members of the underclass, because of their dysfunctional worldview, ignore the economic opportunity blossoming all around them.[9]

These charges, it's crucial to note, represent a significant expansion of the idea of racism. Racism once meant thinking about and treating members of a given race as essentially, biologically, inferior. But such bigotry, as Dinesh D'Souza, author of a thick book on race relations, points out, "has been morally discredited; few people admit to it." To keep the idea of racism alive—and not coincidentally to provide work for civil rights activists—the Left has had to invent a new, amorphous type of racism that "must be inferred," in D'Souza's words, from one's positions on issues.[10] The new racism comes down to this: If you oppose liberal policies, on racial preferences or on anything else that affects blacks, you must be out to harm black Americans. The Democrats' campaign in January 2001 to derail the nomination of John Ashcroft as the nation's new attorney general drew freely on this expansive conception of racism, though liberals couched it in different rhetoric, saying that the former Missouri senator was "insensitive" toward blacks.

A related charge conservatives often hear from liberals is that, whatever they might say, they're really mean-spirited white people whose goal is to make the rich richer at the expense of the poor, the black, and the helpless—especially kids. Such attacks reached a fever pitch after Republicans won the House of Representatives in 1994. "What [conservative Republicans] want to do," President Clinton said, "is make war on the kids of this country."[11] Former Democratic New York governor Mario Cuomo evoked the image of "Republican storm troopers."[12] Another New York Democrat, Congressman Major Owens, went further: "These are the people," he thundered, "who are practicing genocide with a smile: They're worse than Hitler."[13] The domestic policy ideas that the Republicans stand for—limited government, welfare reform, tax cuts, deregulation—don't seem to have all that much to do with Nazism or the Holocaust. But in the political rhetoric of today's liberals, fine distinctions—distinctions of any kind, really—often get lost. Up until recently, protected by a mainstream media cocoon, liberals weren't challenged on such excesses.

::       ::       ::

The Left's effort to push conservative opinions outside the realm of acceptable discourse takes on even greater force in cultural disagreements, like the controversy over how to treat homosexuality. For liberals, fighting for homosexual rights is the moral equivalent of blacks' fight for civil rights, so that anyone who opposes, say, gay marriage or who supports the Boy Scouts' freedom not to hire homosexual scoutmasters is a bigot—end of story. But it's one thing to say that all men are created equal and quite another to hold that all forms of sexual behavior are morally equivalent. The least one can say is that such a contention needs rational argument and not mere assertion.

A conspicuous example of this effort to discredit conservative views on homosexual behavior was the 2000 campaign by gay activists to shut down Laura Schlessinger's Paramount-produced television show. "Dr. Laura," an Orthodox Jew who accepts the biblical proscription of homosexual acts, contends that homosexuals have a right to "respect and kindness" but that homosexual sex is "deviant" behavior. Whatever one thinks about that view, leading religious thinkers and moral philosophers have endorsed it for thousands of years. But that didn't stop gay activists from making Dr. Laura out to be the "Queen of Hate Radio." Their campaign succeeded in pressuring major corporations like Procter & Gamble and American Express to withdraw their prospective ads—in effect endorsing the view that traditional sexual mores are now taboo. Dr. Laura's TV show was canceled after a short run.

One further example: The Claremont Institute, a respected conservative think tank in California, and the National Association for Research and Therapy of Homosexuality set off an enormous controversy when they invited a group of conservative political thinkers and psychiatrists who don't accept the idea that homosexuality is genetically determined—a key tenet of many homosexual-rights activists—to a Los Angeles conference on the legal and medical status of homosexuality. Without bothering to inquire, the Los Angeles City Council rushed to condemn the conference as an exercise in "defamation and demonization." As conference participant Hadley Arkes, a well known Amherst political scientist, later put it, "A moral tradition running back to Athens (yes, Athens) and Jerusalem was now pronounced as nothing less than unspeakable in Los Angeles."[14] The Beverly Hilton Hotel, the original site for the conference, backed out after receiving menacing calls, forcing the organizers to move to a braver hotel. Conference leaders received death threats. Protesters disrupted the proceedings, screaming that the people speaking inside the hall were murderers of homosexuals or the moral equivalent of the KKK.

::    ::    ::

Liberals claim that conservatives who criticize homosexual behavior as immoral or deviant create a "hostile climate" that leads to gay-bashing. Shortly after the brutal murder of homosexual Matthew Shepard by actual gay-bashers, Jonathan Alter of *Newsweek* sought to blame all moral conservatives for the crime. "[J]ust as white racists created a climate for lynching blacks, just as hate radio created a climate for militias, so the constant degrading of homosexuals is exacting a toll in blood," Alter charged. "Discerning clergymen and moralists can hate the sin and love the sinner," he continued, "but by the time the homophobic message reaches the angry guys sitting in the bar, the distinction has been lost."[15]

If all Alter was saying is that conservatives should strive to be civil in making their arguments about homosexual behavior, then he'd find few serious conservative thinkers or politicians who'd disagree with him. His real meaning, though, is that anyone espousing traditional views should just be quiet. Like most of today's Left, Alter rejects Voltaire's famous dictum "I disapprove of what you say, but I will defend to the death your right to say it."

The Left's position on homosexuality is no longer about winning tolerance for it but about getting everyone to celebrate it as just one more perfectly normal sexual lifestyle, something many religious conservatives adamantly reject. The easy assumptions Alter makes are illustrative:

that conservative criticism of homosexual behavior is "degrading," for example, or that the moral teachings of, say, the Catholic Church, are "homophobic"—an expression of mental illness, in other words. British writer Melanie Phillips, no conservative, sees in such casual assertions a breathtaking illiberalism and inversion of traditional values. A "homophobe," she observes, is now "[a]nyone who believes that sexual orientation should remain a private matter and who deplores the intimidation of those who wish to keep it so."[16]

Abortion is another cultural controversy in which liberals simply try to silence conservative views—sometimes quite crudely—and have generally gotten away with it, with the help of their mainstream media protectors. As former Democratic congresswoman Patricia Schroeder put it when criticizing abortion opponents, "We don't want to see that kind of goose-stepping over women's rights."[17] The "hostile climate" charge gets a frequent workout in this context, too. The *Washington Post*'s Richard Cohen, in a 1997 column titled "When Morality Begets Violence," blamed the "language of the anti-abortion movement, a piece of it anyway," with inciting bombings at abortion clinics. "Wherever there is a connection to abortion, there is always the possibility of violence," he claimed.[18] As syndicated columnist John Leo wisely counsels, "Beware of arguments based on climates or atmospheres. Most of them are simply attempts to disparage opponents and squelch legitimate debate."[19]

::     ::     ::

Ironically, the tendency to treat conservative opinions as a form of bigotry and extremism has found its warmest welcome in the seat of liberal learning, which once held sacrosanct the freedom to debate ideas. Obligatory sensitivity sessions inculcating the "correct" attitudes toward feminism, homosexuality, and race; speech codes that punish "inappropriate laughter"; university officials looking away when student activists disrupt a conservative professor's classes; conservative speakers uninvited from campus lectures—by now the litany of college political correctness has become a familiar butt of ridicule, but it has worked to banish or silence anything resembling a conservative viewpoint at our nation's universities. "It's the campus leftists who're the real Torquemadas today," judges author and civil libertarian Nat Hentoff.[20] (Later, we'll see how the Left's control over campus life is starting to weaken.)

Breaking with the media mainstream's silence about this censorship, Hentoff brought to national attention one example that could stand for thousands. A few years ago, a conservative Cornell University student newspaper published a parody of Ebonics—a label given by some academics to various forms of African American speech that a handful of educational theorists and activists ill-advisedly thought should be taught in inner-city schools as the equivalent of standard English. Student activists stole two hundred copies of the offending paper and torched them in a bonfire. "There was no public criticism by members of the administration or the faculty of this transmogrification of the principle of free inquiry," Hentoff complained. When emboldened vandals stole five hundred copies of another edition of the paper and burned them as well, Cornell's dean of students actually stood in front of the bonfire in support with the offending students. A university spokesman, Hentoff reported, called the burning "symbolic"—and added that Cornell respects both the right to publish and the right to protest.[21]

::      ::      ::

It's not just the administrators and student groups on campus who view conservative arguments as beneath contempt. Highbrow philosophers do it too. As far back as the 1960s, neo-Marxist guru Herbert Marcuse anticipated much in today's illiberal liberalism. His Orwellian idea of "liberating tolerance" could serve as the official philosophy of the contemporary liberal Left. Old-fashioned liberal tolerance—freedom of speech, say, or freedom of association—is "repressive," Marcuse argued, since it just props up the old power structure. "Liberating tolerance," on the other hand, "would mean intolerance against movements from the Right, and toleration of movements from the Left." It is, as a Hentoff book title tartly puts it, "free speech for me—but not for thee."[22]

The most influential liberal philosopher of the last thirty years, John Rawls, took a similar tack. Rawls didn't openly endorse Marcusean coercion; he claimed to be a defender of reason and of liberal freedoms. But in his 1993 *Political Liberalism*, he showed himself to be equally willing to silence conservative opinions. Rawls argued that a free and equal society must base its laws only on "reasonable" views of political justice. And then, in a short footnote, he defined "reasonable" in a way that ruled out-of-bounds any arguments that deny a "mature adult woman" the right to a first-trimester abortion. (Rawls backed away somewhat from this assertion in a later paperback edition of the book.)[23]

Political theorist Peter Berkowitz asks the decisive question of Rawls and his many followers, who now dominate the teaching of political philosophy: "What kind of guidance for the negotiation of disagreement in a democracy can be derived from a conception that by fiat proclaims unreasonable and places beyond the pale of public discussion the considered views of many Catholics, Protestants, and Jews, to say nothing of the views of the loyal Democrats who have been made to feel like pariahs in their own party for their principled pro-life positions?"[24] Answer: none.

Even Supreme Court justices have succumbed to this easy, unthinking waving away of venerable conservative beliefs as if they were without merit and beneath debate. The 1996 *Romer* v. *Evans* decision is a dispiriting case in point. In striking down Colorado's democratically enacted constitutional provision that homosexuals or bisexuals should not have special rights over and above the rights guaranteed to every citizen, the court opined that objections to homosexual practices were a form of "animus"—agreeing, in a less vociferous way, with the argument of Dr. Laura's gay-activist critics that no American can have a reasoned objection to homosexual behavior. Judge Robert Bork summed up *Romer*'s remarkable implications: "We are on our way to the approval of homosexual conduct, despite the moral objections of most Americans, because the Court views such moral disapproval as nothing more than redneck bigotry."[25]

What's more, since the Court itself gives no reason for singling out homosexual activity as deserving special protection from moral censure—and only moral censure is at issue, since no one is advocating legal proscription—*Romer*'s underlying logic is even more radical than it first appears. In effect, the decision really implies that *any* moral disapproval of *any* consensual sexual behavior is a form of animus—the 1960s libertine ethos of "if it feels good, do it" institutionalized in turgid legal prose. The Court's 2004 *Lawrence* decision, striking down long-unenforced sodomy laws, has enshrined this understanding of the Constitution. In his *Romer* dissent, Justice Antonin Scalia blasted the Court for "imposing upon all Americans" the anti-traditional views of a liberal "elite class."[26]

The casual way that Rawls and *Romer* dismiss conservative ideas manifests a remarkable self-satisfaction that possesses many in what Scalia calls the "elite class," including those in the old media. They share the spirit of liberal Harvard psychologist Lawrence Kohlberg, whose famous (now hoary) theory of the stages of moral development culminated, comically, with . . . Harvard liberalism! And this unshakable self-complacency reminds us that people don't always (or perhaps even usually) come to the views they hold by study, reason, and reflection.

Fashion and stigma play their parts, too—which is why argument by invective can be so effective. Lytton Strachey used to dismiss views that questioned Bloomsbury's antibourgeois values with a withering, "Oh, *come!*" And many elite communities—Rawls's Cambridge, say, or Manhattan's Upper West Side, or the CBS newsroom—are no different from Strachey's Bloomsbury in this respect: It's presumed that you'll have the correct liberal opinions. "Challenge this presumption, and you'll stop getting invited to dinner parties," reports Westchester-dwelling ex-liberal and bestselling author Harry Stein.[27]

This illiberal approach to political debate went into overdrive with the Left's reaction to George W. Bush's close victory over Al Gore in the 2000 presidential race. Referring to the large swaths of the country that voted for Bush—colored bright red on the newspaper maps—liberal pundit and Clinton and Kerry adviser Paul Begala wrote, "You see the state where James Byrd was lynch-dragged behind a pickup truck until his body came apart—it's red. You see where Matthew Shepard was crucified on a split-rail fence for the crime of being gay—it's red. You see the state where right-wing extremists blew up a federal office building and murdered scores of federal employees: red. The state where an Army private thought to be gay was bludgeoned to death with a baseball bat, and the state where neo-Nazi skinheads murdered two African Americans because of their skin color, and the state where Bob Jones University spews its anti-Catholic bigotry: They're red too."[28] Though Begala later claimed that critics had taken his commentary "out of context," its message is clear: Conservatives are killers.

In seeking to defeat the nomination of John Ashcroft as attorney general, liberals tried to do more than make Ashcroft out to be a racist. Without argument, they sought to relocate the "mainstream" leftward, in order to make any conservative seem well out of it, an extremist. Even ostensible moderate Joe Lieberman exploited this tactic: "On issues ranging from civil rights to privacy rights," Lieberman intoned in voting against his former Senate colleague, "Senator Ashcroft has repeatedly taken positions considerably outside the mainstream of American thinking."[29]

But consider Lieberman's two stated examples: civil rights (read: racial preferences) and privacy rights (read: abortion). Columnist Charles Krauthammer correctly responds, "In a country so divided on these issues, can one seriously argue that opposing abortion and racial preferences is proof of extremism? It would be odd indeed if the minority of Americans who believe in racial preferences and the minority who believe in abortion-on-demand were to define the American mainstream."[30] By his own new standard, Lieberman himself had been just a short while ago "outside the mainstream" on racial preferences, which he opposed, and on partial-birth abortion, at which he expressed discomfort.

::     ::     ::

The 2004 presidential campaign, dominated by the Iraq War and the emergence of the new conservative media, marked what might be the frenzied apotheosis of this illiberal liberalism. "In two hundred years of this nation's political history, there has never been a hate campaign as massive, as nasty, and as personally vicious as the one directed against President Bush," conservative author and FrontPage editor David Horowitz argued. Horowitz's scorching indictment of the Democrats' political rhetoric is worth quoting in full.

> As president, [Bush] has been denounced as a traitor who has "betrayed" Americans, a liar, a corrupt manipulator who misled America and sent its young and innocent to battle in full knowledge that their mission was fraudulent and their deaths needless. It has been charged that the sole reason he sent the young to die was to line the pockets of his corporate Texas cronies. He has

been accused in advance of being responsible for any dirty nuclear bomb that terrorists detonate in the United States. And these are merely the attacks originating with Al Gore and Ted Kennedy before spreading through the Democratic ranks. Not a single Democrat, by the way, has stood up to deplore the reck-lessness of these smears, or to speculate on how such attacks might affect the fortunes of the troops under the President's com-mand.[31]

Horowitz could have added Kerry's baseless charges that President Bush was going to restore the draft and steal senior citizens' Social Security—cynical outright lies. Centrist commentator Morton Kon-dracke, writing in *Roll Call*, had to concede that the Democrats were "well out in front" in the low-blow department.[32] In columnist John Podhoretz's view, the Kerry-Edwards ticket took negative campaigning into "uncharted territory."[33]

Once you left the precincts of party leadership, the Left behaved more thuggishly still in the 2004 election—smashing glass doors and damaging property at GOP headquarters in Arizona and several other states, intimidating voters in line in polling places, and trashing GOP signs across the country. I can attest to the ugly behavior firsthand. After my wife placed a "W." sticker on our car (in a liberal suburban New York neighborhood), we had a door keyed and a window spat on. On one occasion, as she drove our two young children to school, a car full of Bush-haters cut her off violently, screaming obscenities. We removed the sticker. These are the illiberal methods of something other than democrats.

Unfortunately, as Horowitz correctly goes on to note, the main-stream media, instead of fulfilling their role as impartial arbiters of fact, gave shameful attacks like these a free pass. But then, the media elite didn't seem any more troubled by the star treatment meted out at the

Democratic convention to "documentary" filmmaker Michael Moore, whose despicable *Fahrenheit 9/11* implied Bush administration complicity in September 11 and who once likened the Islamofascist thugs killing American civilians and soldiers in Iraq to freedom fighters. This mendacious huckster got to sit next to the party's elder statesmen, among them ex-president Jimmy Carter.

After President Bush's win on November 2, some in the elite media went beyond enabling illiberal liberalism to practicing it. The respected pundit and historian Garry Wills, writing in the *Times*, compared the sixty million people who voted for Bush to jihadists. "Where else do we find fundamentalist zeal, a rage at secularity, religious intolerance, fear of and hatred for modernity?" Wills asked rhetorically. "Not in France or Britain or Germany or Italy or Spain," he answered. "We find it in the Muslim world, in Al Qaeda, in Saddam Hussein's Sunni loyalists. Americans wonder that the rest of the world thinks us so dangerous, so single-minded, so impervious to international appeals. They fear jihad, no matter whose zeal is being expressed."[34] Writer Jane Smiley, posting on the liberal webzine Slate, lamented "the unteachable ignorance of the red states."[35]

::        ::        ::

The liberals' mainstream media–sheltered habit of censoring and discrediting conservative views is a holdover from the 1960s New Left, whose style and ideology left a profound stamp on the Democratic Party and on many who now call themselves liberals. The New Left divided the political world into "the good inside and the monstrous outside," in the words of political scientist Richard Ellis, author of an important study on radicalism in America.[36] The radicals were the good guys working for a radiant future of sexual and political emancipation; the bad guys included not only conservatives, the defenders of a supposedly unjust and oppressive society, but also the fuddy-duddy liberals, whose belief in reason and civility made them weak-kneed accomplices of the irredeemably corrupt conservatives.

If you see politics as a struggle between absolute good and absolute evil, then it's easy, if you're on the right side of history, to start calling your opponents names. "Fascist" was the approved epithet of the 1960s, equivalent to "racist" today or "Communist" in the mouth of Senator Joe McCarthy. It's easy, too, to start rationalizing away unprincipled behavior within your own ranks. "If the other side is a group of barbarians," political theorist Peter Berkowitz says, "it justifies the shameless behavior: 'If we don't cheat, and steal, and lie,' the liberals think, 'then George W. Bush and John Ashcroft are going to be running the country.'"[37]

But politics by invective is a double-edged weapon, because intelligent people will ultimately stop believing these accusations. Now that the proliferation of new media—talk radio, cable television, the blogosphere—is giving conservatives popular forums in which they can challenge and rebut their accusers, illiberal liberalism's political efficacy is eroding fast. "[T]he saturation point has long been reached for hysterical, rote charges about racism, sexism, and homophobia," observes culture critic Camille Paglia.[38] And then the question will be whether the name-callers have any real ideas behind the invective.

We turn now to talk radio, the medium that began the revolt against the old-media regime.

Chapter Three

# Fighting Back: Conservative Talk Radio

**D**rive across the country these days, and you'll never be out of range of conservative voices on the AM dial or satellite radio—Rush Limbaugh's, of course, but also those of Sean Hannity, Laura Ingraham, Dennis Prager, William Bennett, Hugh Hewitt, Larry Elder, Dr. Laura, Michael Savage, Mike Gallagher, Mark Levin, Ken Hamblin, and many, many more, both national and local.

To say that the Right has flourished in the AM talk universe is a big understatement. Democratic senator Byron Dorgan of North Dakota commissioned a study of a week's worth of programming by the nation's forty-four highest-rated AM radio stations and found that they broadcast 312 hours of conservative talk programming, with just five hours of left-leaning shows. Writing recently in *The Public Interest*, political scientist William Mayer noted that of the top twenty-eight talk-radio programs nationwide, eleven—and four of the top five—had conservative hosts; none featured liberals. On local radio, conservative hosts outnumber liberal ones by three to one. "Simply put," Mayer writes, "conservatives dominate talk radio to an overwhelming, remarkable degree."[1]

Political talk radio is now so ubiquitous that it's easy to forget just how recent a phenomenon it is. It owes its existence in large part to

President Ronald Reagan and his innovative Federal Communications Commission. Before Reagan, the FCC's Fairness Doctrine, codified in 1949, required radio (and later TV) stations seeking a license or a license renewal to comply with two conditions: First, they had to cover "vitally important controversial issues of interest in the community served by the broadcaster." At the same time, they had to "provide a reasonable opportunity for the presentation of contrasting viewpoints on such issues." A broadcaster's failure to live up to these terms could result in fines, free airtime for what federal regulators deemed underserved views, and ultimately, loss of license. Regulators wanted to ensure that radio stations, which they saw as public trustees, didn't use their privileged access to a limited broadcast spectrum to pursue partisan agendas.

In fact, the Fairness Doctrine became a powerful weapon for politicians and interest groups to wield against broadcasters who opposed their views. Bill Ruder, a former assistant secretary of commerce in John F. Kennedy's administration, once admitted, "Our massive strategy was to use the Fairness Doctrine to challenge and harass the right-wing broadcasters, and hope that the challenges would be so costly to them that they would be inhibited and decide it was too costly to continue."[2] The Nixon administration did much the same against its perceived on-air enemies. In turn, media critic John Corry points out, special interest groups "would complain that a radio or television station was being unfair to whatever cause they favored. If the station didn't meet their demands, they would turn to the FCC."[3]

Such pressure made radio stations leery about political programming of any kind. Boisterous, wildly opinionated political talk radio in today's sense was out of the question. "There was no such thing as political talk radio because you had the Fairness Doctrine," relates conservative public relations maven Craig Shirley. "If you had the 'Craig Shirley Show,' fully sponsored, and it was an hour-long, right-wing screed, then you had to put on the 'Paul Begala Show' as a left-wing screed for an hour and maybe do it gratis if there was no one to sponsor it."[4] Why risk it? No surprise that in 1980, there were only seventy-five or so stations running talk shows of any kind on the American airwaves. "There was a perverse incentive to only broadcast blandness," observed Bruce Fein, general counsel at the FCC from 1983 to 1984.[5]

Everything began to change in the early 1980s, when Mark Fowler, the libertarian head of Reagan's FCC, told his regulators to stop enforcing the Fairness Doctrine. For Fowler, the doctrine served no public interest and was "chilling to free speech"—as it obviously was, even though the Supreme Court had upheld its constitutionality against a First Amendment challenge in the 1969 *Red Lion* case, involving a Christian radio station that had refused to grant "equal time" to a journalist who had been criticized on air. Moreover, by the 1980s, author and communications industry expert Peter Huber notes, the "old scarcity argument for fairness had been overtaken by the new technological abundance."[6] Cable and satellite television, for example, had brought scores, even hundreds, of new channels. "[T]he interest of the public in viewpoint diversity is fully served by the multiplicity of voices in the marketplace today," a 1985 FCC report sensibly asserted.

In 1987, Reagan's second FCC chairman, Dennis Patrick, officially junked the Fairness Doctrine. Liberals howled. So did some conservatives, among them Phyllis Schlafly, who had leaned on the doctrine in her victorious struggle against the Equal Rights Amendment. An agitated Congress then voted to make the Fairness Doctrine a federal law, which would have strong-armed the FCC into restoring the old regulatory regime. But President Reagan, true to his free-market philosophy of keeping government busybodies out of business, vetoed the bill.

Result: an AM revolution. With the Fairness Doctrine dead, political talk shows, most of them robustly conservative, began to burn up the airwaves. A 1998 study by communications experts Thomas W.

Hazlett and David W. Sosa found that from 1987 through 1995, the share of "informational" AM programming expanded from 4.29 percent to 20.89 percent of the total on-air mix. By 2004, roughly 1,400 stations were devoting themselves exclusively to talk on AM—a stunning seventeen-fold increase from Fairness Doctrine days. More than four thousand talk-show hosts were now broadcasting. Industry magazine *Multichannel News* got it exactly right: Reagan's elimination of the Fairness Doctrine "planted the seeds for partisan talk radio dominated by conservatives."[7] Some of these hosts aren't directly political, it's important to note, but rather Christians with culturally conservative views. Religious radio broadcasting has also exploded in recent years, though it remains largely unnoticed by the mainstream media.

Reagan's move also saved AM radio, nearly defunct by the 1980s, believes *Talkers* magazine editor and publisher Michael Harrison. "There were five thousand AM radio stations out there that couldn't compete against five thousand FM stations playing music," he explains.[8] Talk radio enabled mono AM to compete with stereo FM, since stereo sound mattered little when people were gabbing and not playing tunes.

::     ::     ::

Pruning away the regulatory thickets wouldn't have been enough to unleash the spectacular growth in right-of-center political broadcasting. Conservative talk radio also needed to show that it could draw listeners. Enter a former disc jockey and salesman named Rush Hudson Limbaugh III. "He's the one who created the modern talk-radio phenomenon, so everyone in this business owes him," talk-radio hostess Laura Ingraham admiringly says of Rush. "When he came along, there was no one else like him."[9]

In 1987, the then thirty-seven-year-old two-time divorcé was a relative unknown, broadcasting on Sacramento's KFBK. He had replaced

Morton Downey, Jr. as a host on the AM station and—freed from Fairness Doctrine shackles—sent ratings skyward by talking politics from a stance of unapologetic conservatism. Media entrepreneur and former ABC president Ed McLaughlin, driving through Sacramento one day, liked what he heard and persuaded Limbaugh to come to New York and launch a nationally syndicated show (new satellite technology now made such national broadcasts feasible). McLaughlin proposed a deal to AM stations: They could carry Limbaugh's noon-to-three broadcast for free in exchange for a percentage of advertising revenue, an innovative arrangement later termed the barter model.[10]

On August 1, 1988, the Excellence in Broadcasting network premiered on several dozen struggling AM radio stations across the country, with roughly 250,000 listeners tuning in. Nobody outside the Sacramento area had ever heard anything like the *Rush Limbaugh Show* before. The host's self-confidence, like his girth at the time, was Davy Crockett immense—so over-the-top one had to laugh. "Greetings, conversationalists across the fruited plain," a typical intro would go. "This is Rush Limbaugh, the most dangerous man in America, with the largest hypothalamus in North America, serving humanity simply by opening my mouth, destined for my own wing in the Museum of Broadcasting, executing everything I do flawlessly with zero mistakes, doing this show with half my brain tied behind my back just to make it fair because I have talent on loan from...God. Rush Limbaugh. A man. A legend. A way of life."[11]

But it was Rush's brash conservatism that was really unprecedented on the AM dial. Writer Terry Eastland, a big fan, described the host's philosophy as based on certain bedrock premises: "That all human life has been created by God and is sacred; that God placed man in dominion over nature, including the animals, who do not, strictly speaking, have rights; that no healthy society can dispense with belief in God or the public accommodation of religious practices; that there is a moral law, grounded in religion, by which man's behavior must ultimately be judged; that there are differences in nature between men and women that are relevant to the way in which we should order at least some things—such as our military—in public life; that society should not guarantee equal outcomes but equal opportunity; that governments are instituted to protect the rights of individuals; and that individuals flourish best when government is limited and families are strong."[12]

Limbaugh summed up his worldview in less highfalutin terms. "What I am . . . is anti-liberal. Liberalism is a scourge. It destroys the human spirit. It destroys prosperity. It assigns sameness to everybody. And wherever I find it, I oppose it."[13]

::          ::          ::

That opposition entailed unceasing, reasoned argument. A college dropout, Limbaugh had put himself through a rigorous self-education, mastering an array of issues. Liberal fallacies on economic and social policy, foreign policy, media distortions, intraconservative squabbles—Rush weighed in on it all, and usually at a high level. "Rush is extremely sophisticated, extremely smart," conservative pundit and former Reagan education secretary William Bennett observed back in 1993.[14] "He's very serious intellectually. He knows how to argue *ad finem* and *ad absurdum*."

Outright mockery of leftist nonsense—argument *ad absurdum*—was indeed a crucial part of the Rush mix. Limbaugh's show introduced such sure-to-enrage-liberals features as the "Animal Rights Update," opened by a recording of Andy Williams crooning "Born Free" with sounds of gunfire, explosions, and animal screams mixed in. Through Rush's lens, the NAACP became the NAALCP—the "National Association for the Advancement of Liberal Colored People." Radical pro-abortion feminists were "feminazis." Before Rush, anti-liberal ridicule of this kind—and we'll look at a lot more of it in Chapter Five—was almost unheard of in the media.

Rush's deftly produced, entertaining, and sometimes rude program caught fire. In just a few years, six hundred stations were carrying the show. The number of weekly listeners—astonishingly—surged past fifteen million. Soon Rush was a household name, publishing bestselling books, hosting a short-lived half-hour television show (produced by political consultant Roger Ailes, who'd later go on to run FOX News), touring, and signing up to his newsletter hundreds of thousands of "dittoheads" (as Rush fans, who agreed with him on almost everything, called themselves)—all in addition to his hugely popular daily radio program. "No broadcast persona has so dominated public discourse since Walter Winchell—and Winchell had only fifteen minutes a week, not fifteen hours," *Playboy* opined in 1993, introducing a 14,000-word interview with the host.[15]

Limbaugh has maintained his preeminence ever since, despite well-documented battles with hearing loss; painkiller addiction and a related prosecutorial witch hunt, led by a Florida state attorney, seeking some kind of drug charges against him; a third divorce (Rush's personal life is spotty); and legions of Rush-haters.

::        ::        ::

As his audience grew exponentially, Rush accrued substantial political influence. Such was Limbaugh's sway that President George H. W. Bush, seeking reelection in the 1992 presidential race against Bill Clinton, visited the show (which rarely features guests) in a late appeal to get Republican voters to the polls on election day. After Clinton's victory, *National Review* anointed Rush "Leader of the Opposition."

Limbaugh led a vast new armada of right-of-center talk-show hosts against the Clinton administration's policy prescriptions. Hillarycare went down in defeat thanks largely to talk radio (and researcher Betsy McCaughey's famous *New Republic* article explaining the statist implications of the health care plan, journalist William Kristol's faxes, and lots of conservative direct-mail campaigning). A Kaiser Foundation survey of members of Congress and their staffs found that for 46 percent of them, talk radio was the most influential media source during the health care debate; 15 percent said the *New York Times*, and only 9 percent said television. Veteran conservative activists Richard Viguerie and David Franke underscore the implications: "How far the liberal giants had fallen!"[16]

The Limbaugh armada helped the Newt Gingrich–led Republicans win Congress in 1994, the first time in half a century that the GOP had taken control. "Rush," Harvard political scientist Harvey Mansfield observed at the time, "converted many, many hoverers and legitimized conservatism as a doctrine of the people, not just of businessmen and intellectuals."[17] The GOP gains shocked the Democrats and their allies in the elite press and the academy, but as iconoclast scholar Camille Paglia suggested, anyone "monitoring what was going on on the *Rush Limbaugh Show* with an open mind could not have been surprised."[18] Without talk radio and C-SPAN, Gingrich later recalled, "the classic media elite would have distorted our message."[19]

Limbaugh's political muscle hasn't weakened. In 2000, Rush's backing proved key in securing George W. Bush's decisive victory over John McCain in the Republican presidential primary. One study showed that a one-day-per-week increase in Limbaugh listening correlated with a 45 percent increase in the likelihood a Republican voter would choose Bush instead of McCain.[20] Limbaugh also helped kill Patrick Buchanan's effort to "redefine American conservatism in the image of his father, circa 1939—isolationist, nativist, protectionist," argues historian and journalist Michael Barone. "Rush took Buchanan on, point by point, in his broadcasts in the 1996 and 2000 news cycles," he explains. By speaking directly to Buchanan's obvious "target audience," Barone says, "Limbaugh reduced him to 0.4 percent of the vote in 2000. That's a big difference."[21]

Rush's cultural impact has been equally profound. "He is doing to the culture what Ronald Reagan did to the political movement," William Bennett, who himself recently joined the talk-show host ranks, declared in his early assessment of Limbaugh. "He tells his audience that what you believe inside you can talk about in the marketplace. People were afraid of censure by gay activists, feminists, environmentalists— now they are not, because Rush takes them on."[22] Conservatives at last found their attitudes and beliefs validated and given forceful expression through a powerful media outlet. The forces of political correctness drew back.

Rush proved that conservative talk radio could be profitable as well as influential. *Mediaweek* notes that the *Rush Limbaugh Show* has generated more than $1 billion in revenue since its inception. In the early days, skittish advertisers wouldn't touch it—too controversial. "We had to go out and find advertisers who were fearless, young entrepreneurs, companies that had never been on radio," Limbaugh recently recalled. "And they had to be products I believed in and used."[23]

One was the then little-known beverage Snapple, promoted by Rush as "the official beverage of the Excellence in Broadcasting Network." Thanks partly to the publicity, the Snapple firm has become a beverage industry powerhouse. Limbaugh now has no difficulty enticing blue-chip advertisers like General Motors and Pfizer.

The radio industry being reactive, it didn't take long for executives to seek to imitate Rush's triumph. By the time the Clinton years were in full swing, as we've seen, the radio waves buzzed with voices from the Right. Many of those voices have won huge listening audiences, amplifying the influence of conservative ideas and arguments by orders of magnitude.

Right behind Rush is former Long Islander Sean Hannity, whose three-hour daily blast of hard-nosed conservatism, nationally syndicated for several years now, draws twelve million listeners a week on nearly four hundred ABC Radio Network stations, mirroring the high ratings of the FOX News hour he co-hosts with liberal Alan Colmes. Hannity received the 2004 National Talk-Show Host of the Year award from the annual Radio & Records Talk Radio Seminar and the 2003 Marconi Award for Network/Syndicated Personality of the Year, signs of his rising clout. Though critics lump them together, Hannity and Limbaugh have very different approaches. Unlike Rush, Hannity loves on-air debate, and his show features daily guests, both liberals and conservatives, mixing it up. Bush administration officials, keenly aware of Hannity's authority with his listeners, troop into his studio regularly.

After Hannity, there's Laura Schlessinger, "Dr. Laura" to the nine million listeners who tune in every week to hear her bracing commentary on contemporary mores. Then comes Michael Savage, whose fierce attacks on "red-diaper doper baby lawyers who attended NYU and Columbia" and blistering critiques of U.S. immigration policies pull seven million listeners weekly.[24] Starboard-side commentators such as Neal Boortz, Mike Gallagher, Glenn Beck, G. Gordon Liddy, Bill O'Reilly, Hugh Hewitt, Rusty Humphries, Michael Medved, Laura Ingraham, William Bennett, Larry Elder, and Tony Snow each draw between one and two million listeners a week.

The political views of these hosts, while clearly coming from the right, are far from monolithic. Boortz, for instance, leans libertarian, while Hewitt calls himself center-right, and Liddy is, well, Liddy. Styles differ, too, just as much as between Hannity and Limbaugh. Medved invites the listeners who disagree with him most vehemently to call in and debate. Ingraham lightheartedly covers the entertainment world as well as politics. Gallagher is pleasant in tone but unforgiving in argument. Bennett says his model of on-air conversation "is the Socratic dialogue"—"serious conversation with intelligence, candor and good-will."[25]

And there are many, many more smaller-scale conservative talk-radio hosts too, illuminating local concerns from Boston to San Francisco with perspectives from the right. Though claiming tiny listenerships compared with the big stars, local conservative talk-radio hosts have influence—even on the national level, if they happened to broadcast from the 2004 battleground states. For instance, Scott Hennen's *Hot Talk*, broadcasting on two 5,000-watt eastern North Dakota stations that happened to reach swing state Minnesota, scored election-season interviews with Vice President Dick Cheney, First Lady Laura Bush, and other top-shelf Bush-camp guests. "The White House has been committed to talk radio since day one," explained Hennen.[26]

A smart move, since 22 percent of Americans now claim to get daily news primarily from talk radio, according to a 2003 Gallup poll, and an additional 39 percent tune in several times a week or occasionally. And they're politically informed and active Americans. Studies show that talk fans vote in greater percentages than the general public (73 percent claim to have voted in 2000, according to a *Talkers* survey, compared with 52 percent of the eligible voting population), tend to be college-educated and make good money, read more magazines and papers, and are active in the community. "They're not just passive listeners," Ingraham says. "They're passionate about issues."[27] They're not all hard-core right-wingers, either. About 25 percent of them say they're Republicans, while 53 percent claim to be registered Independents and 12 percent Democrats.

Right-of-center think tanks have taken full advantage of the talk medium to bypass the old media's liberal gatekeepers and gain access to this informed, engaged audience. Every day, right here where I work, for example, Manhattan Institute thinkers get to offer their views on tax policy, crime, culture, and politics on radio shows from New Hampshire to Oregon, and on national broadcasts as well. Fellows at the Washing-ton-based Heritage Foundation collectively do two thousand radio interviews a year. And as we'll see later, talk radio has enabled book publishers to sell conservative books to an eager readership.

The Left has tried its hand at talk, too, but with zilch to show for it. Major-league liberals like Mario Cuomo, Alan Dershowitz, Susan Estrich, and Jim Hightower proved to be ratings poison when hosting their own radio talk shows, all canceled after short periods on the air. The latest, much-publicized effort to boost the Left's radio presence—Air America—has struggled to date (including having some problems paying the bills early on), despite tons of free publicity and a roster of hosts that includes such celebrity liberals as former *Saturday Night Live* writer and author Al Franken, comedian Janeane Garofalo, and rapper Chuck D.

::     ::     ::

What accounts for the remarkable success of conservative talk radio—and the failure of liberals on the airwaves? Why isn't there a liberal Rush Limbaugh? Some on the Left say that it's because liberals are, well . . . smarter. The complexity of their thinking, liberals assert, makes for less thrilling, if truer, listening. Former New York governor Mario Cuomo—whose failed radio show had about a dozen regular listeners—gave canonical expression to this arrogant, self-serving view. Conservatives "write their messages with crayons," he told Phil Donahue. "We use fine-point quills."[28] Unlike the Right, former Colorado senator and Democratic presidential aspirant Gary Hart similarly argued, "the reformer, the progressive, the liberal, whatever you want to call it, doesn't see the world in blacks and whites, but in plaids and grays. There never is a single simple answer."[29] Getting that sophistication across on talk radio in a way that connected with the audience wasn't easy, believed Hart, whose own talk-radio show flopped.

I've got a quick—yes, black-and-white—response to this argument: hogwash. Even if we *were* to grant the premise that conservative talk radio can sometimes be crudely simplistic—a tough charge to make stick against, say, one-time philosophy prof Bennett or former Clarence Thomas law clerk Ingraham, to take just two top hosts—how can anyone plausibly believe the Right has a monopoly on reductive, misleading argument? "For every simple-minded conservative slogan there is an equally vacuous catchphrase on the Left," William Mayer writes in his pathbreaking essay on political talk radio (to which I'm indebted here). Mayer adds, "If the collected works of Rush Limbaugh are unlikely to be published in an academic policy journal, neither would the writings of Jesse Jackson, Al Franken, Jim Hightower, or Michael Moore"—a comparison that flatters the four liberals.[30]

A second explanation that liberals sometimes offer for the conservative domination of the medium is that the super-rich corporate execs who run the radio industry are right-wingers themselves, and keep "progressives" off the air to favor their own corporate-friendly political ideology. Mayer quotes Jeff Cohen, head of the liberal media watchdog group Fairness and Accuracy in Reporting, on this score: "There are a lot of phony excuses for why the right wing dominates, but the most obvious, true explanation is that the management at these stations is conservative."[31]

This contention is no sounder than the liberals-are-smart-conservatives-are-dumb one. We've already seen how radical media types tend to be, and there's no reason to think radio owners as a class would be any different. Even Clear Channel, which syndicates Rush and Dr. Laura and is demonized by liberals, is taking a chance on Air America, putting it on one of its Miami talk stations. If liberal radio can survive in the market, there'll be plenty of radio execs willing to go along. The media universe is obviously not hostile to liberalism.

::     ::     ::

In fact, talk radio is conservative for four major reasons. Entertainment value is one. The top conservative hosts, following Rush's lead (remember, he was a DJ first), put on snazzy, frequently humorous shows. "The successful talk-radio hosts are funny," suggests Kathleen Hall Jamieson, dean of the University of Pennsylvania's Annenberg School for Communication and one of the few academics to study the dynamics of talk radio. "No one wants to listen to three hours of a political diatribe. In fact, no one wants to listen to two hours of a political diatribe. The parody, the asides, the self-effacing humor, the bluster are all part of the packaging that makes the political message palatable."[32] Conservative talk-radio humor, adds *Boston Herald* columnist Don Feder, making a slightly different point, "tends to be the humor of the excluded, with a mordant quality." Middle-class listeners in particular, Feder thinks, "can identify with this laughter from outside that lampoons liberalism's objects of ritual veneration."[33]

Liberals, conversely, tend to be sanctimonious and deadly, deadly earnest, which puts off listeners. Says Ingraham, "They take themselves way too seriously. Most successful radio hosts poke fun at pomposity." The triumph of political correctness on the Left makes it hard for on-air liberals to lighten up (though Air America, with left-wing jokers Franken, Garofalo, and Mark Maron as hosts, is trying).

"The problem for liberals is that their 'movement' extends to virtually every boutique victim group under the sun," comments National Review Online editor at large Jonah Goldberg. "They are terrified of offending anybody in their own massive Coalition of the Oppressed," leaving few targets for humor beyond white Republicans. Goldberg adds, "I guarantee you that if Franken were to make fun of activists from any number of constituencies—gays, Hispanics, blacks, animal rights, environmentalists, fill in the blank—he would be inundated with gripes from his 'base' saying 'that's not funny!' And because he's such a nice, tolerant, Upper West Side liberal, he'd have to listen, apologize, atone."[34] That's one of the central reasons professional liberals—as opposed to professional comics who happen to be liberal, like Franken—aren't very funny.

Fragmentation of the potential left-leaning listening audience is another ratings drag on liberal talk. Political consultant Dick Morris explains, "Large percentages of liberals are black and Hispanic, and they now have their own specialized entertainment radio outlets, which they aren't likely to leave for liberal talk radio."[35] The potential audience for Air America or similar ventures is thus pretty small—white lefties, basically. And keep in mind they've already got NPR, which boasts upward of thirteen million weekly listeners for its highest-rated news programs.

The third reason the Right rules talk radio is the most obvious and most important: blatant liberal bias in the old media. As we saw in the first chapter, not only does the media mainstream flow to the left; the American people also *believe* it's overly liberal. "Liberals, in short, don't need talk radio," argues Mayer. "They have Dan Rather, Peter Jennings, and Tom Brokaw—not to mention NPR. A quite large number of conservatives, however, see network television and their local newspapers as promoting a perspective on national and world affairs that is fundamentally at odds with their own."[36] For conservatives, who outnumber liberals in the country, talk radio—like FOX News and the Internet, as we'll see—helps right the imbalance.

Last, and relatedly, talk radio is inherently populist, the first media forum in which ordinary Joes can actually get a hearing for their complaints about what liberals have wrought in America since the 1960s. "Write a letter to the editor and it takes days to publish, if it is published at all—and then it's often edited," explained the veteran Boston-area radio host David Brudnoy in the *American Enterprise*. "You can get on most talk shows just by dialing the phone."[37] The conservative talk shows helped make it "possible for the vox populi to find expression," neoconservative icon Irving Kristol noted.[38] "It's a long-standing conceit of liberalism that it is the authentic voice of the people," Feder points out. "Talk radio completely spoils this fantasy."

::     ::     ::

Unable to prosper in the medium, liberals, resorting to their trademark illiberalism, have taken to denouncing talk radio as a threat to democracy—an attitude that characterizes the Left's response to new media in general, as we will see in the chapters ahead. Liberal elites "were utterly unprepared for the sudden emergence and swift rise" of the radio talk shows, says Kristol—and it shows in their spluttering anger. Liberal political columnist Hendrik Hertzberg, writing recently in the *New Yorker*, is typically venomous. Conservative talk radio represents "shrill jabber," "viscous, untreated political sewage," and "niche entertainment for the spiritually unattractive," Hertzberg sneers, adding that "the radiocons," as he calls them, "seldom offer analysis or argument." To the ears of the "chronically resentful" conservative listeners, Hertzberg concludes, "political hate talk" is "music."[39]

Liberal commentator Thom Hartmann seems equally unhinged by the presence of Rush, Hannity, and company on the airwaves, seeing in it the harbinger of a rising Reich. Most Americans apparently don't recall "that the single most powerful device used to bring about the SS and its political master was radio," he worries. "As both Nazi Germany and Stalinist Russia learned, a steady drumbeat of a single viewpoint . . . is not healthy for democracy when opposing voices are marginalized."[40] Talk radio is home to "bizarre, bigoted, and often startlingly misinformed diatribes," asserts the "progressive" Center for Media and Democracy, and it "has sustained a discourse of anger, cynicism, and confrontation," laments Georgetown professor Diana Owen, coauthor of *New Media and American Politics*. "What is the attraction of a medium that highlights conflict and discontent" and "shows little respect for societal institutions, leaders, and processes?" Owen wonders incredulously.[41] Talk radio is "democracy run amok," one NBC reporter concluded.[42] So much for a critical citizenry.

Democratic politicians have joined the hue and cry against the talk-radio menace. Smarting from the Republicans' surprisingly strong showing in the 2002 congressional elections, Democratic senator Tom Daschle lashed out at the "radiocons." "What happens when Rush Limbaugh attacks those of us in public life is that people aren't just content to listen," Daschle warned. "People want to act because they get emotional . . . and the threats to those of us in public life go up dramatically, against us and against our families, and it's very disconcerting." Daschle offered no evidence to support his serious charge. That didn't stop him from going on to compare Rush with the Islamic fanatics the country is battling in the War on Terror.[43] A few years earlier, Bill Clinton had basically blamed the Oklahoma City bombing on Rush too. Talk-show hosts "spread hate," Clinton rued. "They leave the impression by their very words that violence is acceptable."[44] Conservative talk = terror.

If some liberals had their way, Congress would reregulate the talk-show "terrorists" out of existence. Back in 1993, for example, the Democrat-controlled Congress mulled "Hush Rush" legislation to restore the Fairness Doctrine. Limbaugh hit the warpath, getting his listeners to deluge Congress with letters and phone calls. So massive was the outpouring that scared legislators ceased their efforts. Yet just last year, New York Democratic congressman Maurice Hinchey again proposed reviving the Fairness Doctrine to protect "diversity of view," and presidential candidate Kerry sent out some signals that he too thought that might be a good idea.

Any reregulation would be anti-democratic and an assault upon free speech. First of all, Rush is "equal time," as he often says. Second, people listen to conservative talk radio because they want to, not because the post–Fairness Doctrine regulatory regime forces them to. "Within the free-market environment, I have flourished," Limbaugh observed in 1993, speaking out against the "Hush Rush" campaign. "I am being blamed for the fact that far more American listeners, exercising their free-market right to choose their hosts and programs, choose me."[45] That is, they chose him and not liberal or purportedly balanced alternatives. Why, though, should politicians punish citizens' perfectly legitimate listening choices?

To claim that "diversity of view" is lacking in 2005, nearly twenty years after the repeal of the Fairness Doctrine, moreover, is downright silly. As OpinionJournal's John Fund editorializes, "Anyone who channel-surfs or roams the Internet knows America isn't suffering from any lack of news sources."[46] Complaints about fairness are really about driving conservative viewpoints from public debate.

Sure, talk radio is partisan, raucous, sometimes overheated. But it's also a source of argument, information, differing perspectives, and, yes, community—"democracy in action," in the words of one writer. It has given the Right in all its varieties a chance to break through the liberal monoculture and be heard. For that, anyone who supports spirited public debate should be grateful.

# Chapter Four

# The FOX Effect

The advent of cable television has been perhaps an even bigger boon to the Right than talk radio—and the biggest boon of all has been Rupert Murdoch's FOX News Channel. Since its 1996 launch, FOX News has provided what its visionary CEO Roger Ailes calls a "haven" for viewers fed up with the liberal bias of the news media—a potentially massive audience, as the success of conservative talk radio showed. In a 1989 address to the Manhattan Institute, Murdoch had predicted that communications technology would soon help free political debate in the televised medium from its "progressive" stranglehold. "In television," he observed, "the increase in the number of channels that's coming will allow a much wider range of voices on the air."[1] With FOX News, Murdoch made his prediction come true.

Watch FOX for just a few hours and you encounter a conservative presence unlike anything on television before 1996. Where CBS and CNN would lead a news item about an impending execution with a candlelight vigil of death-penalty protesters, for instance, at FOX "it is de rigueur that we put in the lead why that person is being executed," senior vice president for news John Moody noted a while back.[2] FOX viewers will see Republican politicians and conservative pundits sought out for meaningful quotations, skepticism voiced about environmentalist doomsaying, pro-life views given airtime, and much else they would never find on other networks.

That FOX's producers and journalists don't all march to a liberal beat has enabled the station to outflank competitors on stories they get wrong or miss entirely because of bias. In April 2002, for instance, the mainstream media rushed to report an Israeli "massacre" of Palestinian civilians in a refugee camp in the West Bank city of Jenin. FOX uniquely—and correctly, it turned out—treated the massacre charge with complete skepticism. "We try to avoid falling for the conventional liberal wisdom in journalistic circles—in this case the conventional wisdom 'Israeli bad, Palestinian good,'" says daytime anchorman David Asman. "Too often ideology shapes the tendency to jump to a conclusion— something we try to be aware of in our own case, too."[3]

Respected FOX anchor Brit Hume has pointed to another story on which FOX led the way: covering the liberal distortions—and general decline—of the *New York Times* under former editor Howell Raines. "Nobody else is going to work that story," Hume explained.[4] Among the news networks, too, only FOX has proved brave enough to expose Jesse Jackson's "charities" as the racialist shakedown operations they clearly are. FOX News (along with investigative journalist Claudia Rosett) also helped uncover the staggering corruption of the UN's $67 billion Oil-for-Food program in Iraq, in which dozens of people, top UN officials among them, took kickbacks. The program also allowed Saddam Hussein to divert billions of dollars into his bank accounts. The liberal media, naively uncritical of the UN, didn't push the story. And whereas other networks boiled CIA adviser Charles Duelfer's 1,200-page survey on Iraq's weapons programs down to variations on the simplistic headline "No WMDs in Iraq," FOX highlighted its important revelations—that those impeding our efforts to disarm Saddam were often those chummily doing business with him, including French and Russian officials, and that the Iraqi dictator had retained a "virtual" WMD program that could jump-start the second sanctions lifted.

One of FOX's most politically significant exclusives came in early 2004, when the network's senior White House correspondent, Jim Angle, broke the story about Richard Clarke's August 2002 background briefing to reporters. Clarke had laid out all the ways that the Bush team had, from January 2001 on, aggressively fought al Qaeda—all ludicrously at odds with his later testimony before the 9/11 Commission and with the contents of his CBS-hyped bestseller *Against All Enemies*, in which he accused the Bush administration of failing to take terrorism seriously before 9/11, despite his warnings. Reporters from other news organizations attended the same briefing Angle had, but no other network or media source went public with Clarke's glaring contradictions, apparently happy to let the anti-Bush frenzy grow. As a colleague soberly put it, "Imagine how the Clarke controversy would have played out without FOX. If it had just been CBS or CNN reporting the story, Clarke would have steamrolled the administration."

True, the FOX News viewer will get more on the Scott Peterson trial or other tabloid controversies than he'd ever possibly need. But FOX also offers a steady diet of serious news, especially on politics. Media writer Ken Auletta—hardly an uncritical FOX admirer—notes in the *New Yorker* that "FOX, to its credit, devotes more time to the workings of government than its rivals do."[5] The *Economist*'s insightful America watchers John Micklethwait and Adrian Wooldridge say, "The network makes a habit of covering the big set pieces of American politics unusually well. Its coverage of the 2002 midterm elections...was significantly better than that of its rivals."[6] In 2004, FOX called every Democratic primary race first, without flubbing one. FOX's tireless Carl Cameron, one of the best-sourced political reporters in the business, regularly scoops the competition.

::      ::      ::

Nowhere does FOX differ more radically from the mainstream television and press than in its robustly pro-U.S. coverage of the War on Terror. After September 11, 2001, the American flag appeared everywhere on FOX, from the lapels of the anchormen to the corner of the screen. Ailes himself wrote to President Bush urging him to strike back hard against al Qaeda. On-air personalities and reporters freely referred to "our" troops instead of "U.S. forces," and Islamist "terrorists" and "evil-doers" instead of "militants." Correspondent Geraldo Rivera, reporting from Afghanistan, sported a gun on his hip and said he'd plug Osama bin Laden if he got the chance. Such open displays of patriotism are anathema to today's liberal journalists, who see "taking sides" as a betrayal of journalistic objectivity.

David Asman demurs. For the free media to take sides against an enemy bent on eradicating the free society itself, he argues, isn't unfair or culturally biased; it is the only possible logical and moral stance. And to call bin Laden a "militant," as Reuters does, is to betray the truth, not uphold it. "Terrorism is terrorism," Asman says crisply. "We know what it is, and we know how to define it, just as our viewers know what it is. So we're not going to play with them: When we see an act of terror, we're going to call it terror." On television news, anyway, FOX alone seemed to grasp this essential point from September 11 on. Says Asman, "CNN, MSNBC, the media generally were not declarative enough in calling a spade a spade."

Veteran newscaster John Gibson, host of FOX's *The Big Story* and author of a 2004 book on anti-Americanism, gets heated when I ask him about the supposed incompatibility of patriotism and objectivity. "I'm an American. I'm not a Brit. I'm not a Frenchman. I do news by an American for Americans," he explains. "Does that mean that I support beating up Iraqi prisoners? No. I'll report it honestly. But I'm not going to pretend that I'm broadcasting on UN TV, like they do on CNN."7

Anchor Shepard Smith used more colorful language in a 2003 interview to make a similar point. "Fuck them," Smith says of the critics. "They are our troops. . . . Waving the flag? [Terrorists] knocked the fucking buildings down, down the street on 9/11. That's where the flag [on FOX's screen] started. We needed a little something to rally around. I admit no apologies. I think the vast majority of Americans are absolutely on board with that. They understand that we are credible journalists, fair and balanced about everything that we do, and still [can] be for our side."8

::          ::          ::

Like conservative talk radio, FOX's very tone conveys its difference from the networks' worldview. "FOX News lacks the sense of out-of-touch elitism that makes many Americans, whatever their politics, annoyed with the news media," maintains media critic Gene Veith. "FOX reporters almost never condescend to viewers," he observes. "The other networks do so all the time, peering down on the vulgar masses from social height (think Peter Jennings) or deigning to enlighten the public about things that only they understand (think Peter Arnett)." For Ailes, who grew up in a blue-collar Ohio community, FOX's anti-elitism is key. "There's a whole country that elitists will never acknowledge," he told the *New York Times Magazine*. "What people resent deeply out there are those in the 'blue' states thinking they're smarter."

This down-to-earth style pervades FOX behind the scenes too, says Gibson. "There's nobody here trying to get on dinner-party lists. I love [PBS's] Charlie Rose. But everybody knows where he gets his guests— the Upper East Side, the Hamptons. The whole outlook on the world, the whole mindset of his show arises out of the East Coast dinner party set. This isn't the way FOX works. It just isn't."

FOX's anti-elitism informs the station's generally respectful treatment of religion, very much at odds with the European-style secularism of the elite media. In a 2003 interview, Brit Hume, who spent years at ABC before going to FOX to anchor its six o'clock news hour, *Special Report*, shared a story from the 1992 presidential campaign that he felt perfectly captured the elite press's contempt for traditional religious faith. Bush the elder had made a campaign stop at a small Christian college in Oklahoma. "You had these fresh-faced kids whose politics probably weren't extremely well formed," Hume recounted. "And the president doesn't visit a Bible college every day. So he comes out onto the platform and they break into extraordinary cheers. And one of my colleagues leans over to me and says, 'Sieg Heil.'"[9]

At FOX, Christians, far from being seen as Nazis, actually receive some respect. "We regularly have on the Reverend Franklin Graham, Dr. James Dobson, and other religious leaders, just as we put on Pat Ireland and Eleanor Clift," explains popular host Sean Hannity, the conservative half of *Hannity & Colmes*. "Most Americans believe in God and have that as their foundation in life. So why shouldn't we have as guests people that they like, respect, and want to hear from?"[10] News boss John Moody is a serious Catholic with a biography of Pope John Paul II to his credit (along with a novel or two), so it's hardly surprising that FOX rarely exhibits the hostility toward Catholicism that one finds elsewhere in the press and broadcast industry.

FOX's anti-elitist tone characterizes above all the *O'Reilly Factor*, hosted by the pugnacious Irishman Bill O'Reilly, the network's, and cable news's, biggest star (and no slouch on talk radio). A self-described "journalistic gunslinger" who proclaims that his is the "only show from a working-class point of view," the former ABC correspondent has become the voice of populist conservativism, taking on the people and institutions "letting Americans down"—a long list that runs from "crooked corporate weasels" and "venal politicians" to "politically correct bureaucrats" and "a media establishment rife with political bias and economically hooked on violence and smut," as the jacket copy of one of his bestselling books vividly puts it.[11]

O'Reilly's hour-long nightly newsmagazine makes for electric television, as hapless left-wing guests enter the "No Spin Zone" only to have their views drubbed mercilessly by the host—after which he politely gives them "the last word." *Economist* reporters Micklethwait and Wooldridge observe, "Why these people keep accepting his invitation is one of the great mysteries of our age."[12]

The *Factor* has become astonishingly influential. When O'Reilly lambasted two Georgia high schools for holding three segregated proms (black, Hispanic, and white) in 2004, for example, the school district, shamed by the attention, voted to end the practice. On a larger scale, O'Reilly's boycott campaign against France for its opposition to the United States over the Iraq War, some believe, may have helped dent French wine sales in this country. FOX now runs a segment, "After the *Factor*," chronicling the show's impact.

The "fair and balanced" approach that FOX trumpets in its slogan is another part of the network's iconoclastic tone. Sure, the anchor or host is often a conservative, but it's clear he is striving to tell the truth, and there's almost always a liberal on hand as well—FOX's programming emphasizes the vigorous exchange of opinions, Left, Center, and Right. "We have an annoying number of liberals on every day," laughs Hannity. "We go to great lengths to balance it out every hour." By contrast, political consultant and FOX contributor Dick Morris notes, "The other networks offer just one point of view, which they claim is the objective and fair one—you get the omniscient anchor and you get the news, as he chooses to give it you, usually with a liberal slant."[13] Not only does the FOX approach make clear that there is always more than one point of view, it also puts the network's liberal guests in the position of having to defend their views, something that rarely happens on the networks.

::     ::     ::

Viewers clearly like what they see. FOX's ratings, already climbing since
the station debuted in 1996, really began to rocket upward after the terrorist attack and blasted into orbit with Operation Iraqi Freedom. "In
the Iraqi war," Dick Morris explains, "the viewing audience truly saw
how incredibly biased the other networks were: 'Turkey did not let us
through, the plan was flawed, we attacked with too few troops, our supply lines weren't secure, the army would run out of rations and ammo,
the Iraqis would use poison gas, the oil wells would go up in flames,
there would be street-to-street fighting in Baghdad, the museum lost its
priceless artifacts to looters'...and all the while, thanks in part to FOX
News, Americans are seeing with their own eyes how much this is crazy
spin." The yawning gulf separating reality and the mainstream media
during the war and its aftermath, Morris believes, "will kill the other networks in the immediate future—to FOX's benefit."

The numbers make clear just how stunning FOX's rise has been.
Starting with access to only seventeen million homes (compared with
CNN's seventy million) in 1996, FOX reached sixty-five million homes
by 2001 and had already started to turn a profit. A year later, profits hit
$70 million and doubled that in 2003. Though CNN founder Ted
Turner once boasted he'd "squish Murdoch like a bug," FOX News has
outpaced its chief cable news rival in the ratings since September 11,
2001, and now runs laps around it. By June 2003, FOX was winning
a whopping 51 percent of the prime-time cable-news audience—more
than CNN, CNN Headline News, and MSNBC *combined*. During
the second ratings quarter of 2004, FOX owned nine of the top ten
highest-rated cable news shows.

The station's powerhouse, the *O'Reilly Factor*, averages around two
million viewers every night, and during Operation Iraqi Freedom the "No
Spin Zone" drew as many as seven million on a given night; CNN's Larry

King, once the king of cable (and the only non-FOX news broadcast in the top ten), has slipped to 1.3 million nightly viewers. Cheery *FOX and Friends* has edged out CBS's *Early Show* in the ratings a few times, despite the fact that CBS is free while FOX is available only on cable and satellite (and not every operator carries it). Covering the 2004 Republican convention, FOX even beat its network competitors in prime time—a first. For President Bush's convention speech, FOX drew 7.3 million viewers, compared with 5.9 million who watched it on second-place NBC. As election returns came in during the evening of November 2, FOX broke its own record, drawing over eight million viewers with its energetic and informed coverage. While the total viewership for ABC, CBS, and NBC News—more than twenty-five million—still dwarfs FOX's viewers, the networks are hemorrhaging. The three network-news programs had one million fewer people watching in late 2003 than they had twelve months earlier. Ten years ago, 60 percent of Americans watched the network news regularly. Now 34 percent do.

FOX enjoys especially high numbers among advertiser-coveted twenty-five- to fifty-four-year-old viewers (more than doubling CNN's ratings for this key demographic), and it is attracting even younger news junkies. As one CNN producer admits, FOX is "more in touch with the younger age group, not just the twenty-five to fifty-four demo, but probably the eighteen-year-olds."[14] Even more attractive to advertisers, FOX viewers watch twenty to twenty-five minutes before clicking away; CNN watchers stay only ten minutes. FOX's typical viewer also makes more money on average—nearly $60,000 a year—than those of its main cable rivals.

Not only conservatives like what they see. A 2004 Pew Research Center survey shows that of the 25 percent of adult Americans who now regularly watch FOX News, 52 percent call themselves "conservative," compared with 36 percent of CNN fans who do so. The station is thus exposing many centrists (30 percent of FOX's regular viewers) and liberals (13 percent) to conservative ideas and opinions they would not regularly find elsewhere in television news—and some of those folks could be liking the conservative worldview as well as the world-class professionalism of the staff (Ailes doesn't hesitate to fire people if they don't have what he wants), the snazzy and bold graphics and production, and the veracity of the programming.

:: :: ::

Even more than talk radio, FOX News drives liberals right off the deep end. Here are just a few (of countless) examples of liberal outrage directed at the network:

> Former vice president Al Gore likened FOX to an evil right-wing "fifth column," and said he yearned to set up a left-wing competitor—as if a left-wing media doesn't already exist.[15] Former Democratic presidential candidate Howard Dean asserted during his campaign that "on ideological grounds" he'd consider using the FCC to break up FOX News.[16] A group of congressional Democrats hinted that legislation might be in the works if FOX didn't end its "unfair and unbalanced" bias toward the Republican Party.

> *Los Angeles Times* editor John Carroll asserted: "If FOX News were a factory situated, say, in Minneapolis, it would be trailing a plume of rotting fish all the way to New Orleans." FOX practices "pseudo-journalism," Carroll charged—sheer right-wing "propaganda."[17] Carroll's media critic at the *Times* bashed FOX as "the most blatantly biased major American news organization since the era of yellow journalism."[18] *Washington Post* media writer Tom Shales called FOX a "propaganda mill."[19] Former CBS News anchor Walter Cronkite claimed FOX has "eliminated journalism."[20]

> Former *Washington Post* ombudsman Geneva Overholser resigned
  from the board of the National Press Foundation to protest its
  awarding Brit Hume the 2004 Sol Taishoff Award for Excellence
  in Broadcast Journalism. FOX News pursues "ideologically connected journalism," Overholser charged, unlike the media mainstream, which "engages in a quest, perhaps an imperfect quest,
  for objectivity."[21] Past recipients of the award include Dan Rather,
  Howell Raines, and NPR's Nina Totenberg, but Overholser apparently had no problem honoring them for excellence.
> Comedian and Air America host Al Franken's bestseller *Lies and
  the Lying Liars Who Tell Them* is one long jeremiad against
  Murdoch's network. So is Robert Greenwald's *Outfoxed*, a documentary film funded by left-wing advocacy groups, so biased
  in its depiction of the network's purported bias—quotes taken
  out of context, deceptive editing, you know the drill—that even
  some liberals criticized it. David Brock's *The Republican Noise
  Machine* argued that FOX is so dangerous that it threatens our
  democracy.
> Leftist groups MoveOn.org and Common Cause filed a spuri-
  ous petition with the Federal Trade Commission that FOX's use
  of its famous "Fair and Balanced" slogan is deceptive advertising and so should be banned. "When a news outlet is allowed
  to blur the lines between opinion and journalism and call it 'fair
  and balanced,' I think it's confusing to consumers of information in this country and it's dangerous to democracy," said Common Cause president Chellie Pingree, echoing Brock.[22]
> 1960s radical and Columbia Journalism School professor Todd
  Gitlin worried that FOX "emboldens the right wing to feel jus-
  tified and confident they can promote their policies."[23]
> "There's room for conservative talk radio on television," allowed
  CNN anchor Aaron Brown, the very embodiment of the elite

journalist. "But I don't think anyone ought to pretend it's the *New York Times* or CNN."[24]

> *Detroit News* columnist Laura Berman feared that with FOX "something hard-edged and unpleasant is creeping into American culture"; she longed for the days when everyone watched *Today*, a "soothing" show "designed to appeal to a great swath of Americans."[25]

> Time Warner chairman Dick Parsons denounced FOX as "crazy people exchanging views."[26]

Wow, liberals really hate FOX, don't they?

The reason, believes the Media Research Center's Tim Graham, is that FOX News is doing something different from talk radio, whatever Aaron Brown might say—something no media outlet has ever done. "Limbaugh could analyze the 'news' but didn't really make it," Graham explains. "FOX arrived as a professional news organization, uttering the media's own forgotten mantras about fairness and balance, and defined 'news' as something different than what the elite consensus says it is. Democrats receiving contributions from communist China could now be news, for example." Adds Graham, "Even the opinion shows are breaking news on FOX."[27]

It's a bit much to hear liberals, who've given us such objective purveyors of news as CBS News and Raines's *New York Times*, shouting, "Media bias! Media bias!" Still, is there something to the charge that FOX practices partisan pseudo-journalism? An examination of their evidence leaves you pretty unpersuaded.

As Exhibit A, liberals gleefully cite a 2003 study from the University of Maryland's Program on International Policy Attitudes (PIPA) that proves—or so they claim—that FOX drums right-wing falsehoods into its viewers' brains. "Those who receive most of their news from FOX News are more likely than average to have misperceptions" about the

Iraq War, the study authors claimed, especially compared with those who got their news from NPR or PBS. The supposed misperceptions, according to PIPA? That Saddam Hussein had been involved with al Qaeda; that weapons of mass destruction had turned up in Iraq; and that world opinion had supported the United States in its war effort.[28]

The study is worthless. For starters, two of the "misperceptions"—that Saddam had dealings with bin Laden's Islamofascist fanatics and that WMD had turned up in Iraq—weren't as wrong as the study made them out to be. As the *Weekly Standard*'s Stephen F. Hayes has been documenting since early 2003, a host of circumstantial facts suggests that Saddam had started to forge an anti–United States terror front with bin Laden in the 1990s, culminating in a possible Prague meeting between World Trade Center suicide bomber Mohammed Atta and Iraqi intelligence figures a few months before September 11.[29]

As for those missing WMD, while no stockpiles had been discovered, by the time the study appeared, U.S. weapons sleuths in Iraq had found reference strains of various bioweapon agents in the home of an Iraqi defense scientist, a prison lab complex for testing bioweapons on human guinea pigs, scores of chemical and bioweapon recipes and equipment, and lots, lots more nefarious activity. But then, by "weapons of mass destruction," snarled right-wing controversialist Ann Coulter in one of her better ripostes, "what liberals mean is: missiles pointed at Washington, D.C., with their 'Ready to Fire' lights blinking ominously and their warhead payloads clearly marked 'Weapons of Mass Destruction! Next Stop, The Great Satan America!'—basically what you might see on an episode of the original *Batman* TV series."[30]

Unlike the liberal press, FOX gave these two ongoing stories full attention in 2003 (it interviewed Hayes at length, for instance). And it's still covering them better than its elite competitors. When a sarin-filled weapon exploded in Baghdad in May 2004, FOX led with the story for a whole day. The mainstream media barely noticed, prompting the *New*

*York Times*'s William Safire to pen a scathing column: "Sarin? What sarin?" "You never saw such a rush to dismiss this as not news," Safire complained.[31] Safire's own paper buried the sarin story on page 11. As discussed above, FOX covered the Duelfer report's revelations on Saddam's virtual WMD program thoroughly. So who is misinforming whom?

The *Wall Street Journal*'s James Taranto noted another ruinous problem with the study shortly after it came out. "Here are some demonstrable untruths the survey *didn't* ask its subjects about," Taranto wrote:

> > President Bush said Iraq posed an "imminent" threat.
> > Bush claimed Iraq had bought uranium from Niger.
> > America's intervention in Iraq was unilateral.

If these were the claims queried—all of which liberals repeated, mantra-like, despite their falsehood (Bush argued that we had to act against Iraq *before* danger became imminent, and asserted that British intelligence believed Saddam had *sought* uranium in Africa, while many nations joined the United States in the "coalition of the willing" to defeat the Ba'athists)—PBS viewers probably would have registered a higher level of misperceptions than FOX viewers. In any case, asked Taranto, "would not a fair survey have included examples of the misperceptions on both sides?" PIPA's study was "pure propaganda," he concluded.[32]

The other evidence FOX-haters raise to bolster their case that the network twists the news to benefit Republicans is a series of "incriminating" memos from news chief Moody, leaked to the makers of *Outfoxed*. Let's look at three that had liberals buzzing angrily (I've cleaned up a few typos that appeared in the original memos).

> > March 25, 2004. "There can be no proof more compelling and
> > visual of what Palestinian suicide bombers are all about than
> > the pitiful sight of a teenager frantically cutting away the bomb

vest he was wearing in order to save his life. 'I don't want to die,'
he said. Without willing dupes, this barbaric practice can't continue. Let's not overlook that story today, even if the tape has
been out there for a while. As is often the case, the real news
in Iraq is being obscured by temporary tragedy. The creation of
a defense ministry, which will be run by Iraqis, is a major step
forward in the country's redevelopment. Let's look at that, as
well as the death of a U.S. soldier in a roadside bombing."

> April 4, 2004. "Into Fallujah: It's called Operation Vigilant
Resolve and it began Monday morning (NY time) with the U.S.
and Iraqi military surrounding Fallujah. We will cover this hour
by hour today, explaining repeatedly why it is happening. It won't
be long before some people start to decry the use of 'excessive
force.' We won't be among that group. The continuing carnage
in Iraq—mostly the deaths of seven troops in Sadr City—is leaving the American military little choice but to punish perpetra-
tors. When this happens, we should be ready to put in context
the events that led to it. More than six hundred U.S. military
dead, attacks on the UN headquarters last year, assassination
of Iraqi officials who work with the coalition, the deaths of
Spanish troops last fall, the outrage in Fallujah [i.e., the mutila-
tion of charred U.S. corpses]: whatever happens, it is richly
deserved."

> May 5, 2004. "Thursday update: the pictures from Abu Ghraib
prison are disturbing. They have rightly provoked outrage. Today
we have a picture—aired on Al Arabiya—of an American
hostage being held with a scarf over his eyes, clearly against his
will. Who's outraged on his behalf? It is important that we keep
the Abu Ghraib situation in perspective. The story is beginning
to live on its own momentum. The facts of the story may develop
into the need to do much more in the days ahead. For the

moment, however, the focus appears to be changing to finger-pointing within the administration and how it plays out as an issue in the presidential campaign."[33]

How are these bracing directives—and the others made public are quite similar—evidence of dark, untruthful partisanship? They show Moody pushing FOX to avoid the blame-America-first-and-always war reportage of the mainstream media, steadying the FOX stance that terrorists aren't "freedom fighters" or "militants" but unambiguously evil, and responsibly seeking background and context. That FOX's critics view the memos as proof of the network's Republican agenda and disregard for the truth says more about the moral confusion of today's Left than it does about FOX's supposed distortions. The memos are far less compromising than the one ABC News political boss Mark Halperin fired off weeks before the 2004 election, instructing his troops to go easy on candidate Kerry's untruths (see Chapter One). What's more, FOX employees "are free to call me or message me and say, 'I think you're off-base.' Sometimes I take the advice, sometimes I don't," insists Moody.[34] "I flatter myself by thinking I'm the supervisor that people can disagree with," he informed industry mag *Broadcasting & Cable* a few years ago. "You can't be too imperial in news."[35]

Furthermore, if FOX is a Republican "fifth column," why did it break the story of George W. Bush's youthful DUI just four days before the 2000 presidential election? Karl Rove certainly didn't phone in *that* request. The revelation, many believe, nearly cost Bush the election. In 2004's presidential race, FOX pollsters consistently underestimated the president's support; in their final poll before the election, FOX had Kerry winning by a couple of points—one of the only polls to show the Democrat on top.

A 2003 study (a serious one this time) from a UCLA political scientist and a University of Chicago public policy professor sheds brighter and truer light on the bias question at FOX. It found Brit Hume's *Special Report*—FOX's most straightforward newscast—far more "fair and balanced" than other media outlets when it comes to asking think tanks for their opinion. *Special Report* cited 372 liberal think tanks and 367 conservative ones between 1998 and 2003. From 1990 to 2003, by contrast, CBS *Evening News* cited 815 liberal think tanks and 283 conservative ones. ABC's *World News Tonight* and NBC's *Nightly News* proved only slightly fairer than CBS, the study found.[36]

There's no question, of course, that FOX News is more conservative than CBS or PBS or CNN, or that some of its most forceful personalities—O'Reilly, Hannity, Hume on the air; Ailes, Moody, and perhaps Murdoch behind the scenes—belong to the Right. FOX's programming reflects the network's founding mission to correct the bias toward the Left virtually everywhere else in the news media. But to call FOX a "propaganda machine," given its comparative balance and proven professionalism, is just silly. CBS *MarketWatch* media editor Jon Friedman (whose surprise over Bush's reelection I had a little fun with earlier) hits exactly the right note: "The success of FOX is not the result of FOX being right-wing. It's because they did such a good job of reaching out to the right-wing TV audience."[37]

The fair and balanced observer will hear in the hysterical complaint and angry foot-stamping of FOX's liberal critics baffled frustration over the loss of the liberal monoculture, which, I've argued here, long protected the Left from debate—and further, from the realization that its unexamined ideas are sadly threadbare. What the illiberal liberals really object to is *any* conservative presence, however fair-minded, in public debate.

::     ::     ::

And on that score, FOX is giving liberals even greater reason to worry. FOX's success has led some of its news competitors to ape it by becoming friendlier to conservatives—a phenomenon that media watchers call the FOX Effect. If not for FOX, for example, it is unlikely that MSNBC would be running *Scarborough Country* (hosted by former Florida congressman Joe Scarborough) or CNBC the *Dennis Miller Show*, two programs that feature right-leaning hosts and scores of conservative guests.

"I *know* I wouldn't be here if it wasn't for FOX," acknowledged the forty-one-year-old Scarborough in a 2003 interview. Airing at 10 PM, *Scarborough Country* clearly patterns itself after the *O'Reilly Factor*, right down to the similar opening editorial segment: Scarborough dishes "The Real Deal"; O'Reilly lays down his "Talking Points." "People around here call me Little O'Reilly," Scarborough says, though it's not the host's height—at 6'4", he's as tall as the lanky FOX star—but his genial, softer style and perhaps his slighter, though respectable, ratings (250,000 or so a night, an eighth of O'Reilly's draw) that earns him the diminutive.[38]

Scarborough once performed in a punk rock band and seems irreverently at home in popular culture; his politics, though, are unambiguously conservative. He sees his entertaining, informative show as a corrective to the liberal bias of the elite media. "If I can help tip the scales at MSNBC, which is currently more down the middle, I think that's a victory," he explained. Whether *Scarborough Country* tips those scales—the show did replace Phil Donahue's ill-fated liberal opinion hour on the station, canceled after just six months—or not, it happily provided the occasion for one of the most withering anti-anti-Bush putdowns in recent memory. Asked to remark on Michael Moore's winning of the Palme D'Or at the 2004 Cannes film festival for the mendacious *Fahrenheit 9/11*, guest Christopher Hitchens pounced: "Speaking here in my capacity as a polished, sophisticated European, it seems to me the laugh is on the polished, sophisticated Europeans. They think Americans are fat, vulgar, greedy, stupid, ambitious, and ignorant, and so on. And they've taken as their own, as their representative American, someone who embodies all those qualities."[39]

The FOX Effect has radiated beyond cable to broadcast news. The Baltimore-based Sinclair Broadcast Group (SBG) is explicitly modeling its news division on FOX's. In late 2002, SBG began feeding its affiliates a seventeen-minute national and international news report that strives to be "fair and balanced"—company CEO David Smith even uses the FOX catchphrase. Conservatives don't have to worry about liberal spin at SBG. The news report actually boasts an opinion segment called "Truth, Lies, and Red Tape" that runs stories that "Brokaw, Rather, Jennings, and Aaron Brown don't want viewers to hear," declaimed SBG vice president Mark Hyman.[40]

The news segment, again like FOX, is proudly anti-elitist. Sinclair stations aren't "in the regions of the cultural elite who look down on the 'little people,'" Hyman tells the conservative webzine NewsMax, referring to the fact that most SBG affiliates operate in Bush-voting "red" states. "I think that is good for us, because the folks who live in the red sections of the country are the ones most starved for a balanced newscast."

The swiftly expanding SBG is now the nation's largest independent group owner of stations and the eighth-largest network based on revenues. The company posted a net profit of $24 million in 2003, with sales of $739 million, a CNN/*Money* report noted. SBG owns or manages sixty-two stations, giving it potential access to a quarter of the American television audience. The news broadcast currently reaches five million viewers per evening. Small wonder vice president Dick Cheney gave Sinclair an exclusive interview at the outset of the 2004 presidential campaign.

Despite such success, Sinclair had barely blipped on the blue states' radar before April 2004, when it ordered its eight ABC affiliates not to run a *Nightline* broadcast that featured anchor Ted Koppel reading the names of hundreds of U.S. soldiers killed in Iraq as their images flashed on the screen. "The action appears to be motivated by a political agenda designed to undermine the efforts of the United States in Iraq," SBG said, defending its controversial order, which liberals and some conservatives, including Arizona senator John McCain, vehemently criticized.[41] "If they wanted to do a program on, Is the cost of this war in human life worth it, and discuss that issue and explain the benefit of what [the U.S.] is doing and what the cost has been and allow people to comment on it, that public debate we will welcome," responded Sinclair general counsel Barry Faber. "But without any context and any discussion of why we're there and why these lives are being sacrificed, it will unduly influence people."[42]

An even greater controversy ensued in October 2004, when SBG said it would require its stations to broadcast *Stolen Honor: Wounds That Never Heal*, a controversial documentary in which seventeen former Vietnam POWs charge that John Kerry's antiwar activities after returning from active duty betrayed them and America. A Kerry spokesman went Tony Soprano on Sinclair: "Listen, they better look out there at Sinclair Broadcasting. . . .I think they are going to regret doing this, and they better hope we don't win."[43] After Democrat-controlled public pension funds threatened shareholder lawsuits, Sinclair blinked, and decided against having its stations run the film in its entirety—a partial victory for the illiberal liberals.

The U Network is yet another example of the FOX Effect. Debuting on at least 150 university campuses via closed circuit in the fall of 2004, this college-only network aims to challenge MTV, whose university feed currently shows on more than 700 U.S. campuses. Rejecting MTV's reflexively left-wing politics, the U Network (TUN, for short) runs a news program that gives equal time to Republican politics and military-themed reality shows. During the 2004 presidential race, it broadcast a weekly documentary series covering George W. Bush's reelection bid. "MTV is doing a fair job of covering Kerry," TUN founder Shane Walker told the *Los Angeles Times* in late August 2004. "Hopefully, we can fill that niche with the president."[44] "We are trying to be less biased," operations coordinator Cass Burt emphasized in a FOX News interview. "We believe in the intelligence of our audience to rely on their own judgment and come to their own conclusions."[45]

TUN promises not only fairer political coverage than MTV but also less vulgar programming. "They've dumbed down," Walker says of MTV. "But we're going to change it."

::      ::      ::

Even before the FOX Effect kicked in, conservatives were benefiting from cable television. A quarter-century ago, Brian Lamb—a former Department of Defense public relations man, Richard Nixon campaign aide, journalist, Hill staffer, and cable television pioneer—decided that he'd had enough with the way the old media covered politics. Lamb launched C-SPAN, a public-affairs network (subsidized by other cable channels) that "puts a camera on the political process," as he matter-of-factly describes it.

Starting out with just $450,000 in capital, four employees, and access to only 3.5 million homes, Lamb's brainchild has grown into a $40 million yearly empire, with 255 full-time employees working at three television stations, ten Internet sites, and a radio station. C-SPAN's television reach now extends to an estimated eighty-seven million households. Though Nielsen doesn't record ratings for the commercial-free network, one in five cable viewers claims to tune in at least once or twice a week. Cable industry publication *Multichannel News* recently described C-SPAN as a "Washington, D.C., institution and so much a part of the political fabric... that it can almost be viewed as a fourth branch of the federal government."

On C-SPAN, viewers can watch congressional wheeling and dealing gavel-to-gavel—sans editorial filter. "The whole place is organized around the no-stars philosophy," explains co-COO Susan Swain. "There's an absence here of overinflated egos." With no bigwig liberal anchor to frame the news, C-SPAN gives Republican pols a fair chance to get their message out directly to the American people. "You never hear a voice-over or a sound bite on C-SPAN," praises political thinker Harvey Mansfield. "In a voice-over," he reasons, "the network reporter gives the gist of a speaker's statements in his own words, and then often illustrates his interpretation with a punch phrase actually taken from the speaker. The emphasis is the reporter's, and the speaker, who may well be the president of the United States, becomes a character in the reporter's story—and thus a witness to the reporter's moral and intellectual superiority." C-SPAN's willingness to let "politics appear as it is," cutting through media bias, Mansfield concludes, "is deeply practical, as it helps us examine the business of our common life."[46]

One conservative leader who instantly grasped the Brokaw-Jennings-Rather–bypassing potential of C-SPAN was a young Republican congressman from Georgia: Newt Gingrich. In the mid-1980s, the firebrand reformer began exploiting the "special order" time at the end of the House of Representatives' working day, when members who haven't gone home can take turns speaking on whatever moves them. In the past, pols would use special orders only if they wanted to enter something officially into the congressional record. Otherwise, why blab to an empty chamber? But C-SPAN's neutral eye recorded the special orders, just as it did everything else that went on publicly in Congress. Gingrich and his allies thus could use the speaking time to get their principled conservative message out to the network's viewers across the nation—a small number in the 1980s, but they were political junkies who always voted.

The strategy worked: As C-SPAN's audience grew, so did Gingrich's influence, until he famously spearheaded the Republican takeover of the House in 1994 (with some not inconsiderable help from Rush Limbaugh, as Chapter Two showed). "The key thing is that Gingrich went where the audience was," noted political scientist Stephen Frantzich. "He recognized that the minority had limited access to the mainline media."[47]

C-SPAN also televises myriad academic talks and panel discussions held at various think tanks, including starboard-leaning ones like the Heritage Foundation and the American Enterprise Institute. The benefit to the conservative cause is unarguable. "If one were to go only by the descriptions offered by the likes of Maureen Dowd," writes National Review Online's Jonah Goldberg, "you'd expect a notorious 'neocon' think tank like the American Enterprise Institute to be full of Roman centurions drinking wine out of goblets, sloshing it over their war maps." C-SPAN, by contrast, Goldberg argues, shows the think tank for what it really is: a place "full of fairly nerdy policy geeks having very serious arguments about very serious things. Seeing that is healthy for everybody."[48]

C-SPAN's *Booknotes*, running from 1989 to the end of 2004, offered authors the rare television experience of talking about their work at great length and was just as politically balanced as the rest of C-SPAN. Lamb himself hosted the show, perfecting an almost Zen-like detachment and neutrality toward his guests. "I feel it's very important that it not be about me, that it's about the author," Lamb once averred.[49] "The intent—though Lamb doesn't boast of it—is to educate," Mansfield says.[50] In recent years, *Booknotes* featured neoconservative elder Irving Kristol, end-of-history scribe Francis Fukuyama, author and editor Adam Bellow, literary critic Jeffrey Hart, columnist Michelle Malkin, historian Victor Davis Hanson, Nobel economist Milton Friedman and his wife, Rose, and many other leading conservatives. If viewers wanted to encounter conservative reflection in depth on the tube, *Booknotes* was the place to go.

C-SPAN will continue to cover the book industry with *Book TV*, running all weekend on C-SPAN II, the network's second television channel. Lamb also will host a new interview show, *Q & A*, which replaces *Booknotes* on Sunday night. It will include occasional discussions with authors about their new books.

∷    ∷    ∷

In sum, a right-leaning news and culture junkie could flick across the television channel array these days and never feel alone—a far cry from even a decade ago, when the media news universe remained monolithically liberal and biased against the Right.

And that's even before he starts laughing—our subject in the next chapter.

# Chapter Five

# South Park Anti-Liberals

**T**he news isn't the only place on cable where conservatives can sometimes feel at home. Lots of cable comedy, while far from traditionally conservative, is fiercely anti-liberal these days, which as a practical matter can amount nearly to the same thing. We'll meet several of the leading representatives of this new comedic spirit in this chapter. For readers put off by cursing or vulgarity, prepare yourself: These comedians like to offend.

The number-one example of the new anti-liberalism is *South Park*, Comedy Central's hit adult cartoon series, whose heroes are four crudely animated and impossibly foulmouthed fourth-graders named Cartman, Kenny, Kyle, and Stan. Now in its eighth season, *South Park*, with nearly three million viewers per episode (one recent half hour garnered 4.4 million), is Comedy Central's highest-rated program, credited by many with putting the network on the map.

Many conservatives (including Brent Bozell) have attacked *South Park* for its exuberant vulgarity, calling it "twisted," "vile trash," and a "threat to our youth." Conservative critics should pay closer attention to what *South Park* so irreverently jeers at and mocks. As the show's co-creator Matt Stone sums it up, "I hate conservatives, but I really fucking hate liberals."[1] Stone freely acknowledges that he and fellow thirty-something Coloradoan colleague Trey Parker are "more right-wing than most people in Hollywood"—though, he cautions, that's partly because Hollywood types are so out there on the Left. "We're just not like Alec Baldwin," he says.[2]

*South Park* sharpens the iconoclastic, anti-PC edge of earlier cartoon shows like *The Simpsons* and *King of the Hill*, and spares no sensitivity. The show's single black kid is called Token. One episode, "Cripple Fight," concludes with a slugfest between the boys' wheelchair-bound, cerebral-palsy–stricken friend Timmy and the obnoxious Jimmy, who wants to be South Park's leading "handi-capable" citizen (in his own cringe-inducing PC locution).[3] In another, "Rainforest Schmainforest," the boys' school sends them on a field trip to Costa Rica, led by an activist choir group, "Getting Gay with Kids," which wants to raise youth awareness about "our vanishing rain forests." Shown San José, Costa Rica's capital, the boys are unimpressed:

> *Cartman* [holding his nose]: Oh my God, it smells like ass out here!
>
> *Choir teacher*: All right, that does it! Eric Cartman, you respect other cultures this instant.
>
> *Cartman*: I wasn't saying anything about their culture, I was just saying their city smells like ass.

But if the city is unpleasant, the rain forest itself is a nightmare: the boys get lost, wilt from the infernal heat, face deadly assaults from monstrous insects and a giant snake, run afoul of revolutionary banditos, and—worst of all—must endure the choir teacher's New-Agey gushing: "Shhh! Children! Let's try to listen to what the rain forest tells us, and if we use our ears, she can tell us so many things." By the horrifying trip's end, the boys are desperate for civilization, and the choir teacher herself has come to despise the rain forest she once worshiped: "You go right ahead and plow down this whole fuckin' thing," she tells a construction worker.

The episode concludes with the choir's new song:

> There's a place called the rain forest that truly sucks ass.
> Let's knock it all down and get rid of it fast....
> You only fight these causes 'cause caring sells.
> All you activists can go fuck yourselves.

As the disclaimer before each episode states, the show is so offensive "it should not be viewed by anyone."

Another episode, "Cherokee Hair Tampons," ridicules multiculti sentimentality about holistic medicine and the "wisdom" of native cultures. Kyle suffers a potentially fatal kidney disorder, and his clueless parents try to cure it with "natural" Native American methods, leaving their son vomiting violently and approaching death's door:

> *Kyle's mom*: Everything is going to be fine, Stan; we're bringing in Kyle tomorrow to see the Native Americans personally.
>
> *Stan*: Isn't it possible that these Indians don't know what they're talking about?
>
> *Stan's mom*: You watch your mouth, Stanley. The Native Americans were raped of their land and resources by white people like us.
>
> *Stan*: And that has something to do with their medicines because...?
>
> *Stan's mom*: *Enough*, Stanley!

One of the contemporary Left's most extreme (and, to conservatives, objectionable) strategies is its effort to draw the mantle of civil liberties over behavior once deemed criminal, pathological, or immoral, as satirized in a brilliant *South Park* episode featuring a visit to town by the (unfortunately, all too real) North American Man-Boy Love Association, the ultra-radical activist group advocating gay sex with minors.

*NAMBLA leader* [speaking at a group meeting attended by the *South Park* kids]: Rights? Does anybody know their rights? You see, I've learned something today. Our forefathers came to this country because they believed in an idea. An idea called "freedom." They wanted to live in a place where a group couldn't be prosecuted for their beliefs. Where a person can live the way he chooses to live. You see us as being perverted because we're different from you. People are afraid of us, because they don't understand. And sometimes it's easier to persecute than to understand.

*Kyle*: Dude. You have sex with children.

*NAMBLA leader*: We are human. Most of us didn't even choose to be attracted to young boys. We were born that way. We can't help the way we are, and if you all can't understand that, well, then, I guess you'll just have to put us away.

*Kyle* [slowly, for emphasis]: Dude. You have sex. With children.

*Stan*: Yeah. You know, we believe in equality for everybody, and tolerance, and all that gay stuff, but dude, fuck you.

A similar theme characterizes "The Death Camp of Tolerance," perhaps *South Park*'s sharpest send-up. This comedic exercise in political theory at once sneers at spurious anti-discrimination lawsuits and excoriates the modern liberal quest to replace the democratic ideal of toleration, which implies moral judgment and limits, with the enforced acceptance, even celebration, of all "lifestyle" choices, however extreme—a very different notion, ultimately corrosive of any social order.

The boys' homosexual teacher, Mr. Garrison, discovers that new laws
protect him from workplace discrimination—and just might make him a
wealthy man, if only he can get the school to fire him for being gay. In a
hypertolerant environment, though, that turns out to be a tall order. Seeking to provoke the school authorities, Mr. Garrison introduces his fourth-
grade class to his new "teacher's assistant," the thickly mustachioed,
heavily muscled Mr. Slave, who struts in wearing a pink shirt, black
leather vest and boots, and a police hat. When the class gets too rowdy,
Mr. Garrison kicks his scheme into motion: "That does it! I will not put
up with foolishness in my class! It's time for punishment!" He pulls out
a paddle and spanks . . . Mr. Slave. The children stare openmouthed.

Stan and Kyle complain to their well-meaning parents about this
bizarre display. But they don't get the supportive response they
expected. Instead, the adults accuse them of being "discriminators" and
decide they need a visit to the "Museum of Tolerance," which puts visitors through absurd sensitivity training exercises similar to those
prevalent on many university campuses these days. Eventually, the
boys wind up interned in an intensive "tolerance camp."

Meanwhile, the parents, guilty over their kids' "discriminatory" attitudes, want to give Mr. Garrison the Courageous Teacher of the Year
award, and arrange for a ceremony at the Museum of Tolerance. The
school embraces the idea. Mr. Garrison is flummoxed: He can't seem
to offend anyone but the children!

At the ceremony, Mr. Garrison enters rodeo-style, bucking on Mr.
Slave's back. The crowd at first appears disturbed, but after a man in
the audience hollers, "So courageous!" everyone claps wildly. Their outrageous performance failing to offend the parents and school officials
sufficiently, the teacher and his assistant launch into an obscene gay-
themed comedy routine.

Again: initial stunned silence, then applause.

Mr. Garrison has had enough. "God damn it," he yells, "don't you people get it?! I'm trying to get fired here! This kind of behavior should not be acceptable from a teacher!" An audience member robotically replies, "But the mus-e-um tells us to be tol-er-ant." Garrison: "Look, just because you have to tolerate something doesn't mean you have to approve of it! If you had to like it, it'd be called the Museum of Acceptance! 'Tolerate' means you're just putting up with it! . . . Jesus Tap-dancing Christ!"

Mr. Garrison never succeeds in getting fired, but common sense more or less prevails.

::     ::     ::

*South Park* regularly mocks left-wing celebrities who feel entitled to pontificate on how the nation should be run. In one notorious parody, made in just several days during the 2000 Florida recount fiasco, loud-mouth Rosie O'Donnell comes to town to weigh in on a kindergarten election dispute involving her nephew. Mr. Garrison, again showing some good sense, dresses her down: "People like you preach tolerance and open-mindedness all the time, but when it comes to middle America, you think we're all evil and stupid country yokels who need your political enlightenment. Just because you're on TV doesn't mean you know crap about the government."

A recent celebrity mark was lampooned even more brutally: actor, producer, and liberal advocate Rob Reiner (Meathead on the old *All in the Family* show). The boys briefly take up smoking after witnessing a puerile school-organized anti-smoking "rap" performance—until the school guidance counselor busts them and calls their folks. Rather than pointing the accusatory finger at themselves or the kids, though, the adults blame the local tobacco company, a displacement of responsibility that the boys, who don't want to face punishment, initially go along with. Reiner, a leading anti-smoking activist, gets wind of the situation and, seeing it as a perfect opportunity to pummel Big Tobacco, sweeps into South Park to spread *his* "political enlightenment."

The episode, "Butt Out," perfectly captures the Olympian arrogance and illiberalism of liberal elites. Overweight and sweating profusely, Reiner crowds into a booth with the boys in the darkened town bar, seeking to draft them into a sleazy plan to frame the local tobacco company for selling cigarettes to minors. Interrupting his pitch, Reiner begins to sniff violently in the air, detecting a faint whiff of cigarette smoke. He zeroes in on the source: a man wearing a "Buds" beer cap, quietly enjoying a beer and a smoke at the bar.

*Rob Reiner:* Oh my God! [He emits a loud hacking noise, but doesn't get the smoker's attention.] Excuse me!

*Buds Man:* Yes?

*Rob Reiner* [indignantly]: Would you mind putting that death stick out?!

*Buds Man:* But, uh, this is a bar.

*Rob Reiner:* Isn't smoking illegal in bars here?

*Bartender:* Not in Colorado.

*Rob Reiner:* Oh my God! What kind of backward hick state is this!?

*Buds Man:* Look, man, I work fourteen hours a day at the sawmill. I just got off work and I need to relax.

*Rob Reiner:* Well, when *I* relax I just go to my vacation house in Hawaii!

*Buds Man* [getting irritated]: I ain't got a vacation house in Hawaii!

*Rob Reiner:* Your vacation house in Mexico, then, wherever it is! Look, you are putting my life and these boys' lives in danger by smoking that in here. And I'm not gonna tolerate it! I will end smoking in bars in Colorado! There will be no more smoking here!

Cartman is predictably awed by Reiner: "Dude, he just goes around imposing his will on people. He's my idol." But the rest of the gang moves to thwart the celebrity's nefarious plans. Kyle and Stan eventually confront Reiner at a town meeting: "You just hate smoking, so you use all your money and power to force others to think like you," Kyle charges. "And that's called fascism, you tubby asshole." Stan is equally incensed: "It wasn't the tobacco companies' fault that we smoked. It was our fault, us! We should all take personal responsibility instead of letting fat fascists like him tell us what to do!" The boys' commonsense argument wins the day.

In a 2004 interview, Parker and Stone expanded on just how much they loathed Reiner and his ilk. "People in the entertainment industry are by and large whore-chasing drug-addict fuckups," Parker noted. "But they still believe they're better than the guy in Wyoming who really loves his wife and takes care of his kids and is a good, outstanding, wholesome person. Hollywood views regular people as children, and they think they're the smart ones who need to tell the idiots out there how to be." Offered Stone, "In Hollywood, there's a whole feeling that they have to protect Middle America from itself. . . . And that's why *South Park* was a big hit up front, because it doesn't treat the viewer like a fucking retard."[4]

Parker and Stone's disgust with celebrity politics is at the core of their uproarious big-screen puppet movie *Team America: World Police*, released in October 2004. Chronicling the adventures of a crack U.S. anti-terrorism squad, the film pokes some fun at American over-zealousness in fighting terror. In Paris, for instance, Team America—whose pulse-pounding theme song shouts, "America, Fuck Yeah!"—takes out a group of Islamists carrying a suitcase nuke but in the process accidentally obliterates the Eiffel Tower, the Louvre, and a puppet who looks a lot like the late French deconstructionist philosopher Jacques Derrida. Yet there's no mistaking the movie's true villains: the Islamist fanatics, North Korean madman Kim Jung Il, who supplies them with WMD to detonate simultaneously around the globe in a "9/11 times 1,000"—and on almost equal bad-guy footing, Hollywood's antiwar liberals.

Led by a creepy Alec Baldwin, the Film Actors Guild (or FAG, for short) is a despicable apologist for the terrorists. It's all our fault the terrorists lash out, you see, Baldwin solemnly explains after a bomb explodes in Panama, killing scores of innocents. Eventually duped into assisting Kim with his nightmarish plans—he only wants peace and understanding, they claim —the actors of FAG clash with Team America in a bloody firefight as the countdown to detonation proceeds. Before it's over, the heroes dispatch—via gunfire, flame, martial arts, and sword—Tim Robbins, Susan Sarandon, Helen Hunt, George Clooney, Martin Sheen, Sean Penn, Janeane Garofalo, and several other lefty celebrities, stopping Kim's apocalypse with only a heartbeat to spare. Oh, yes: A corpulent, mustard-smeared Michael Moore straps on a suicide vest and blows up Team America's Mount Rushmore headquarters.

Team America's newest recruit, actor-turned-spy Gary, sums up the film's central political message with breathtaking anatomical crudity. The world, the marionette says, divides into three types of people: "dicks" (aggressive American right-wingers), "pussies" (peacenik liberals), and "assholes" (terrorists). The dicks can sometimes be obnoxious and thickheaded, all right, and the pussies help keep them in check from time to time, but you need the dicks to deal with the assholes, who will otherwise ruin everyone's lives. And pussies can become *such* pussies that they edge perilously close to being assholes themselves. Got that? If you think about it, it's a surprisingly conservative worldview, shocking vulgarity aside.

"We wanted to deal with this emotion of being hated as an American," Parker elaborated. "That was the thing that was intriguing to us, and having Gary deal with that emotion. And so, him becoming ashamed to be a part of Team America and being ashamed of himself." Eventually, Parker concludes, Gary realizes that he isn't an asshole— and that America has "this role in the world as a dick. Cops are dicks, you fucking hate cops, but you need 'em."[5]

The dour Left hated *Team America*, as you'd expect. Here are some whiny comments posted on the Democratic Underground website right after the flick opened:

"Those guys lost me years ago, when they trashed rain forest preservation and biodiversity."

"It's a propaganda film—the title wants to make close-minded people think America is so good for being 'World Police.' Oh geez, we're in a lot of trouble."

"They poke fun at liberals BIG TIME!!! Nothing against ANY right-wingers, ONLY LIBERALS!!! Liberals are the butt of the joke & are even the villains in this. Oh, & all the liberals die a horrific death in this. TOTALLY bias [sic]! I mean, c'mon. How can they NOT have [a] Bush puppet? I mean, he's so much a character that needs to be mocked. This film was very mean spirited IMO [in my opinion]. My friend said I didn't get it. That it was an extreme right wing edge to it & that was the joke.... Trey Parker & Matt Stone have sold out BIG TIME!"[6]

In its knee-jerk leftism, Hollywood has also long looked down on corporations and the business world in general, as we noted in Chapter One; on occasion, *South Park* gleefully bucks the trend. In "Butt Out," for instance, the tobacco company executives are models of reason and decency, in pointed contrast to Reiner's nasty anti-smoking activists. And in an earlier, even more robustly pro-capitalism entry, a "Harbucks" coffee chain arrives in South Park, to initial resistance but eventual acclaim as everyone—including the local coffeehouse's owners—admits its bean beats anything previously offered in town. "Big corporations are good," Kyle tells the town meeting deciding Harbucks's South Park fate. "Because without big corporations we wouldn't have things like cars and computers and canned soup." Stan adds, "Even Harbucks Coffee started off as a small, little business. But because it made such great coffee, and because they ran their business so well, they managed to grow until they became the corporate powerhouse it is today. And that is why we should all let Harbucks stay." It's worth noting that Matt Stone's father is a semiretired economics professor.

*South Park* even exhibits a socially conservative streak from time to time. In one deftly crafted episode, Stan's parents Randy and Sharon decide to get divorced. Randy swings by in his fancy new red sports car to pick up his devastated son, and tries to explain.

> *Stan's father*: Your mother and I still care about you and your sister, but we just don't like being around each other anymore.
>
> *Stan*: Well . . . I don't like being around my sister anymore. Does that mean I can leave her too?
>
> *Stan's father*: Well, no, because *you're* family. You can't just leave family. You have to stick with family no matter what.
>
> *Stan*: But you and mom are family. How come you can just split up?

Randy is momentarily taken aback, and Stan pounces: "You know what I think? I think that when you and mom got married you became family. And now that you are, you shouldn't be able to leave her any more than I can leave my sister." Randy, panicked, drops Stan back off at home. "You know that *nothing* is more important to me than you, right, Stan?" he says platitudinously, and peels off.

A little later, Stan quarrels with his mother's aggravating new boyfriend, Roy. Sharon seeks to reassure her distressed boy. "Stanley, you know you're the most important thing to me, right?" she says, echoing Randy. "If that's true," Stan replies, "then get back together with dad for me." Mom answers coldly: "Now, Stanley, you have to understand how divorce works. When I say you're the most important thing to me, what I mean is: You're the most important thing after me and my happiness and my new romances." All's well that ends well, however: Stan tricks his parents into sleeping together in his tree house; their love rekindled, mom and dad decide to reunite.

The show has mocked pro-choice extremism, and expressing even the slightest objection to abortion is even rarer in the entertainment industry than positive portrayals of business. During the show's second season, Cartman's mother, Liane, decides to abort her son, then in the third grade. She goes to the Unplanned Parenthood Clinic:

> *Liane*: I want to have . . . an abortion.
>
> *Receptionist*: Well, we can do that. This must be a very difficult time for you, Ms. . . .
>
> *Liane*: Cartman. Yes . . . uh—it's such a hard decision, but I just don't feel I can raise a child in this screwy world.
>
> *Receptionist*: Yes, Ms. Cartman—if you don't feel fit to raise a child, then abortion probably is the answer. Do you know the actual time of conception?
>
> *Liane*: About—eight years ago.
>
> *Receptionist* [processing]: . . . I seee, so the fetus is . . .
>
> *Liane*: Eight years old.
>
> *Receptionist*: Ms. Cartman, uh . . . eight years old is a little late to be considering abortion.

*Liane*: Really?!

*Receptionist*: Yes—this is what we would refer to as the "forti-eth trimester."

*Liane*: But I just don't think I'm a fit mother.

*Receptionist*: Wuh . . . But we prefer to abort babies a little . . . earlier on; in fact, there's a law against abortions after the *second* trimester.

*Liane*: Well, I think you need to *keep your laws off my body*.

*Receptionist*: Hmmmmm. Tsk, I'm afraid I can't help you, Ms. Cartman—if you want to change the law, you'll have to speak with your congressman.

*Liane* [rises from the chair]: Well, that's exactly what I intend to do! Good day!

Liane eventually beds the then president Bill Clinton to try to get him to change federal abortion law. "Well, okay, Mrs. Cartman, I'll legalize fortieth-trimester abortions for you," the sybaritic Clinton drawls, postcoitus. But when Liane discovers, to her horror, that the word "abortion" means termination of life—and not the same thing as "adoption," as she had mistakenly thought—she abandons her lobbying and reconciles with her child.

::      ::      ::

Parker has observed that any time an episode's primary aim is social criticism, rather than laughs, "those shows weren't very good." It's better, he says, to let the commentary "come out of a natural place."[7] But there's no doubting that *South Park*, joining a long tradition that runs from Aristophanes to Tom Wolfe, exemplifies the essence of satire—"the comic as weapon," as social thinker Peter Berger describes it in his book on the comic imagination.[8] Satire, Berger writes, has four criteria: fantasy (often grotesque), a firm moral standpoint, an object of attack, and an educational purpose. *South Park* meets all four.

In addition to the examples of comedic assault we've already looked at, *South Park* has satirized the 1960s counterculture (Cartman has feverish nightmares about hippies, who "want to save the earth, but all they do is smoke pot and smell bad"); sex ed in school (featuring the Sexual Harassment Panda, an outrageous classroom mascot); hate-crime legislation; immigration; and much more. Conservatives do not escape the show's satirical sword—gun-toting rednecks, phony patriots, and Mel Gibson have been among those slashed. But there should be no mistaking the deepest thrust of *South Park*'s politics. Parker and Stone have made their show not only the most obscenity-laced but also the most hostile to liberalism in television history.

:: :: ::

An anti-liberal worldview is also strongly present in non-animated cable comedy. Until quite recently, Comedy Central also played host to *Tough Crowd with Colin Quinn*, a late-night chatfest featuring a revolving panel of stand-up comics, where the conversation—on race, sex, terrorism, war, and other topics—was anything but politically correct. Some of *Tough Crowd*'s top comics, including the gruff and likeable Quinn, regularly upbraided the Left for its anti-Americanism and its stifling PC piety. *Tough Crowd* followed Jon Stewart's popular and ingenious *Daily Show* (which has a far more liberal bent), and for a time retained a respectable chunk of Stewart's audience—an impressive feat, since the show was up against ratings giants Letterman and Leno. It went on "hiatus" in late 2004, but its key performers are involved in numerous other Comedy Central projects, and the network is looking to revive the series in a retooled format in 2005.

The Brooklyn-born, Irish-American Quinn, forty-four, a former anchor on *Saturday Night Live*'s "Weekend Update," an MTV host, and a FOX News fan (he dubs CNN "Al Jazeera West"), can be Rums-feldesque in his stand-up comic riffs, like this one deriding excessive worries about avoiding civilian casualties in Iraq: "This war is so polite," he grumbles. "We used to be *Semper Fi*. Next, we'll be drop-ping comment cards over Iraq saying, 'How did you hear about us?' And 'Would you say that we're a country that goes to war sometimes, often, or never?'"9

Unabashedly pro-American, Quinn views Michael Moore and other antiwar activists with scalding contempt. He opened one *Tough Crowd* show with a piece on how Moore would have portrayed World War II. Against a documentary-style backdrop of grainy black-and-white images of U.S. Marines landing in Normandy, Quinn solemnly began his voice-over: "Here come the pawns in the American corporate anti-socialist party striking at the German people, landing these GM-made boats on the shores of France, polluting the environment and doing col-lateral damage." Pausing momentarily for dramatic effect, he contin-ued, Moore-like self-righteousness seeping into his voice. "This attempt at world domination when we weren't even attacked by Germany but by Japan just lets you know that the Roosevelt administration and Churchill have ulterior motives....And though Hitler has killed six million Jews, we've killed many Germans, so who are we to say that we're better than them? The Germans are fighting us fiercely because we're trying to tell them that our culture of no gas chambers is better than their culture. Who are we to judge? We should look at our own flaws, and maybe set up some sanctions against Hitler until he decides to stop mass-murdering people."10

Quinn, unsurprisingly, has lots of fans in the U.S. military. He and other Comedy Central regulars are USO tour veterans who played to the troops in Iraq and Guantanamo in 2003. "It was a blast," he tells me. "The troops love it when someone is willing to come over and give them a bit of relief."

At its undomesticated best, *Tough Crowd* matched serious topics with irreverent humor. Consider a segment, "Fallen Star," that focused on the mainstream media's treatment of Pat Tillman—the young NFL player who turned down a $3.6 million contract with the Arizona Cardinals to fight, and die, for his country in Afghanistan. It was shortly after Tillman's funeral, and Quinn was livid. "What kills me," he says, leaning on the set's pool table, looking around at the three seated comics joining him for the show, "is that the *New York Times* did this big thing on Pat Tillman's funeral and . . . oh, no, wait, that's right, they didn't write anything on it." The elite media silence signaled a troubling contemporary attitude, Quinn felt. "It's so unhip to say, hey, this guy was a hero—it's in bad taste, it's too nationalistic. . . . You can't say he's a hero, because that sounds like fascism or something."

An important point. But *Tough Crowd* never stayed solemn for long. Guest Greg Giraldo (a Harvard law grad turned successful stand-up) put in his two cents: "Not only was he a hero," Giraldo noted, poker-faced, "but he really did something amazing. In this day and age, when too often the image one gets of athletes is that they're these overpaid, arrogant, flashy babies, Pat Tillman reminds us all that there still are—white athletes."

Such ethnic and racial gibes were common fare on the show. Another segment looked at the disturbing rehabilitation among black, Hispanic, and even white youths of the N-word—"nigger." Comedian Todd Lynn, who is black, wasn't so troubled, saying "context" was all-important—that is, it was okay for minorities to use the taboo word but not whites. Quinn was having none of it. "The word is used so much in the culture now, it's on album covers and in songs," he said with agitation. "So if the word is going to be out there, it can't be just 10 percent of the population that can use it—either everybody says it or nobody." Again, though, the seriousness was swiftly punctured. Willowy (white) comedian Lynne Koplitz offered, "Sometimes you have to use the word. If I don't say it, I don't know my doorman's name, so how am I supposed to get his attention?" Everyone, Todd Lynn included, cracked up.

This kind of politically incorrect repartee had the liberal press fretting. *New York* magazine described the *Tough Crowd* comics as "boorish," "offensive," and "sinking to new lows"—far removed from the traditional New York–style (i.e., liberal, guilt-ridden, psychoanalysis-saturated) comedy of Woody Allen.[11] The *New York Times* accused the *Tough Crowd* comics of being racist troglodytes. A liberal Houston paper says Quinn is "a man of the people—the blue-collar, oft-racist, misogynist people, that is."[12]

These charges make Quinn furious. "That epitomizes what's wrong today with most of the media," he gripes. "Comedy is supposed to be about the truth, but too often it just goes after the permissible targets—the nonexistent Klan, the Christian right, and so on. This isn't to say they don't deserve their slams, too, but everybody should get it—it's fucking comedy. There's an incredible double standard."[13] *Tough Crowd* regular Nick Di Paolo agrees. "Political correctness has run amok," he says. "It's astonishing—the scope and definition of the word 'racist,' for example, gets wider every year, so that if you're white, and speaking about other races in a way that's not completely positive all the time, you're automatically a bigot."[14]

Many of the comedians on *Tough Crowd* were black or Hispanic, and it's easy to imagine them having taken offense at the razzing they received, particularly when it came from white ethnics like Quinn, Di Paolo, or Pete Correale, another knife-elbowed Italian-American comic who appeared on the show. But they took the verbal abuse and gave it right back, equal citizens in a kind of comedic republic.

Quinn came up with idea for the show while arguing politics and culture late into the night, no holds barred, with other comedians at the "comics only" table at the Olive Tree, a restaurant located above

New York's Comedy Cellar on MacDougal Street. "There was much funny stuff at the table that was closer to reality than the bullshit I was often hearing on stage, with all its fake compassion and nonevidentiary ideas about life," Quinn recalls. "I wanted to bring that to TV." Not that viewers should have taken any of it too seriously. "We're comedians, and we're honest, but we're not the Brookings Institution," he says laughing.

::          ::          ::

Quinn isn't Comedy Central's most anti-liberal comic by a long shot. Former Bostonian Di Paolo, a two-time Emmy nominee for comedy writing (*The Chris Rock Show*), called one of "the best comedians" working today by Quinn and a "genius" by liberal comedian and Air America host Janeane Garofalo, easily takes that honor. An unabashed admirer of William F. Buckley and the *New York Post*, Di Paolo, the driving force behind Comedy Central's *Shorties Watchin' Shorties* cartoon, tells me forthrightly, "You won't find any Noam Chomsky on my bookshelf." Justifying his right-leaning politics, the comic, who hails from a blue-collar Italian family, has said, "In this day and age where right is wrong and up is down, it seems like there's no absolutes anymore"—and he refuses such relativism.

Di Paolo's hard-nosed topical comedy places him in the long line of those author and former *New York Post* editor Gerald Nachman labels "the rebel comedians": Mort Sahl, Lenny Bruce, Bill Hicks, and Robert Klein, among others.[15] But whereas the rebel comedians usually directed their fire at bourgeois conventions, Di Paolo targets the orthodoxies of the modern Left.

As in this signature number: "Everybody wails about how they're portrayed on TV, whether it's blacks or women. Political correctness is just making it ridiculous. Even my people, the Italians, are politically correct now, which we were never known to be. We don't like the way we're portrayed on *The Sopranos*. I say, if you want to complain how Italian people are portrayed on TV, why don't you stop those Olive Garden commercials. I'd rather be portrayed as a mob boss who owns a strip club and cheats on his wife than some guy who takes some guys from Italy to the Olive Garden."[16]

And this one: "I like the state of Texas, because they're giving out the electric chair like it's coupons. They've fried like thirty people in the last two months in Texas. And there's a lady in Texas on TV going: 'We're giving too many people the death penalty.' That's bullshit. More people died from air bags last year in the country than from the death penalty. [To Texas lady]: Would it make you feel better if we put these rapists in a Lexus and drove it into a tree? [In effete voice]: 'It's cruel and unusual.' Well, do it more, and it won't be so unusual."[17] As Di Paolo says, he's "insensitive."

Along with their ongoing Comedy Central work, *Tough Crowd*'s politically incorrect comics have revivified New York City's stand-up scene, moribund by the end of the 1990s after thriving in the 1980s. There are "more full-time [comedy] clubs than there were even at the peak of the 1980s boom," *New York* magazine points out—and it's guys like Di Paolo and fellow anti-liberal shock comic and Comedy Central regular Jim Norton who are packing them in, both at older venues like the Comedy Cellar and at new ones like the Laugh Lounge.[18]

College students throng their performances. "I do see some shock on their faces—it's as if they've never heard anybody speak their mind so directly in public before," Di Paolo tells me. "And why would they? You can't get more politically monolithic than college campuses these days," he says. But despite the shock, the college crowd roars with laughter. The incorrect comedy offers a liberating release for students whose left-wing professors seek to impose on them the "right" thoughts about race and sex, making such topics all but undiscussable except in terms of the prescribed dogma.

Benefiting from the growing public thirst for anti-PC humor is rising comic star Julia Gorin, whose "Republican Riot" stand-up routine has played to packed houses at New York's Don't Tell Mama cabaret. Gorin also tours the country with The Right Stuff Comedy, a troupe of right-leaning comics led by former TV comedy writer Eric Peterkofsky. "The only fertile ground to harvest, the only envelopes to push, and the last frontier of comedy will come from the Right," she tells me confidently.[19]

Gorin doubles as a journalist, with op-eds for the *Wall Street Journal*, the *New York Post*, and the *Washington Times* and appearances on FOX News and Bill Maher's *Politically Incorrect* to her credit, but her real love is stand-up. A conservative Jewish woman mocking Islamists, she indeed pushes some envelopes. "The spokesman for the religious police of Saudi Arabia," runs one provocative joke, "recently informed us that the Barbie doll is in fact Jewish. Yeah, Barbie's Jewish. Because, you know, anything that's decadent and Western is necessarily Jewish. So a Michigan-based, Arab-owned company has come out with Middle Eastern Barbie. Her name is Razanne and she's very modest: She's covered from head to toe, she's got no curves, and when she bumps into Jewish Barbie . . . she explodes." Here's another politically incorrect number: "Between schoolkids in California being forced to dress like Muslims and engage in Islamic prayer for three weeks, and American-born kids at bilingual schools reciting the Pledge of Allegiance in Spanish every day, do you realize what's next for American schoolchildren? Islamic prayer in Spanish."

Gorin had started out as a less political comic, but after a few years of trying "to be a sweetheart," she now wants "to kick people in the ass." "The world's stakes became too high, and I felt I had a mission, particularly since I found that it really was possible to translate serious and complex ideas into accessible jokes," she explains.

Someone else who speaks his mind, indoctrinators be damned, is Dennis Miller—*Saturday Night Live* alum, five-time Emmy winner, stand-up comic, former *Monday Night Football* analyst, and host of CNBC's *Dennis Miller Show*. After September 11, 2001, Miller surprisingly came out as a vocal Republican sympathizer—one of precious few in Hollywood.

Miller's move to the right began in the 1990s, partly out of disgust with the liberal response to Mayor Rudolph Giuliani's successful crime-fighting revolution in New York City. "When I kept hearing liberals equating Giuliani with Hitler—that's when I really left the reservation," Miller explained to the *American Enterprise*. "Even before 9/11, I'd travel to New York and say, 'Wow, this city certainly seems to be running better,'" he recalled. "Giuliani is the kind of leader I admire. When it's five below zero and you arrest somebody to get him inside and off the street—that's not something Hitler would do. It made me realize that I was with the wrong group if that's what Hitler looked like to them."[20]

The attacks of September 11, 2001, truly transformed Miller's political allegiances. "I'm left on a lot of things," Miller said in late 2003. "If two gay guys want to get married, I could care less. If a nutcase from overseas wants to blow up their wedding, that's when I'm right. [September 11] was a big thing for me." Liberals, Miller explained, had nothing to offer post–September 11. "They said, 'Well, we're not going to protect you, and we want some more money.' That didn't interest me."[21]

From that point on, Miller became an unashamed fan of President Bush. "Bush had the balls to start something that's not going to be finished in his lifetime," Miller observes. "The liquidation of terrorism is not going to happen for a long time. But to take the first step? Ballsy." The secular Miller also admires Bush's deep Christian faith. "In this messed-up world, I like seeing my president pray," he says. "This is an infinitely complex world and at some point one has to have faith in one's religion. I find it endearing that President Bush prays to God and that he's not an agnostic or all atheist. I'm glad there's something higher that he has to answer to."[22] Miller has even campaigned with Bush, crediting W. for making him "proud to be an American again" after the "wocka-wocka porn guitar of the Clinton administration."[23]

Needless to say, this kind of talk hasn't won Miller a lot of support on the Left Coast, or among liberal elites in general. Their typical line: Miller *used* to be funny; now he's an unfunny right-wing maniac—"the last thing we need more of on television," warns *New York Times* critic Caryn James.[24]

The "Right" Miller debuted professionally in the 2003 HBO stand-up comedy special *The Raw Feed*, where the comic relentlessly derides liberal shibboleths. In his stream-of-consciousness rants, whose cumulative effect gets the audience roaring with laughter, Miller blasts the teachers' unions for opposing vouchers, complains about the sluggish work habits of government workers ("ironically, in our highly driven culture, it would appear the only people *not* interested in pushing the envelope are postal employees"), and attacks opponents of Alaskan oil drilling for "playing the species card."

Miller's hawkish stance on the War on Terror has become central to his humor.

> Dismissing the effectiveness of UN weapons inspectors in the run-up to the Iraq War, he says, "Watching the UN in action makes you want to give Ritalin to a glacier."

> On war opponent France, he's acid: "The French are always reticent to surrender to the wishes of their friends and always more than willing to surrender to the wishes of their enemies" and "The French, you might as well gas up the dinghy and go fishing with Fredo because you are dead to me, okay? You know something? These pricks are now putting—they're putting swastikas on our flag in France. You've got all those boys buried

in Normandy. And after we had the good taste to chisel the armpit hair off the Statue of Liberty you gave us, you know something, I always thought that tint was oxidized copper. Little did I know it was green with envy."

> He is unapologetic about the Iraq War: "I wish there was a country called al Qaeda and we could have started the war there, but there wasn't. And Hussein and his punk sons were just unlucky enough to draw the Wonka ticket in the asshole lottery."

> On complaints about racially profiling Arabs, he's contemptuous: "As for what many are calling racial profiling in the aftermath of September 11, well, get ready to be pissed off, you ACLU-Fucking-Morons, we're dealing with a massive threat and limited manpower, so you want them to check everybody out equally? Sure, fine okay, but let's at least compromise and put the Swedish dwarf a little further down the list than the Iraqi explosives expert carrying a Belgian passport with more eraser marks on it than Kid Rock's trig final."[25]

Miller continues to display this edgy conservative streak on his CNBC show, which pulls in between 200,000 to 300,000 viewers a night. That's a decent bump up in the struggling network's audience share for its 9 PM time slot from pre-Miller days.

The *Dennis Miller Show* blurs—perhaps to a greater degree than any show in television history—what one critic calls "the sacred line between news and entertainment."[26] The host will career from a humorous monologue on the day's events ("Democratic candidate John Kerry underwent surgery to repair a torn rotator cuff; it's a repetitive stress injury caused by years of constantly raising and then lowering his hand while voting in the Senate") to a serious discussion with military historian Victor Davis Hanson to mugging with the show's pet chimp (a tribute to the original *Today*, which also featured a simian cast member) to shooting the breeze about various controversies with a three-member "varsity panel," whose makeup has included conservative firebrand David Horowitz, Harvard Afro-American Studies prof Henry Louis Gates, comic actor Martin Short, blogger Mickey Kaus, and liberal *West Wing* scribe Lawrence O'Donnell, among others.

News purists howl, but Miller's hybrid hour makes for riveting television. After all, where else could one tune in and see, say, comedian Dana Carvey, referring to himself as a "radical centrist," mocking liberal activist attorney Gloria Allred? "Silly, sexy lady," the manic Carvey kept repeating as Allred, in full blustering-left-wing-righteous-indignation mode, tried (unsuccessfully) to argue for gay marriage as a constitutional right. Debates on the show aren't typically that chaotic. In fact, since the host is so well informed, viewers might learn a thing or two while enjoying a few laughs. Listening patiently to a boost-the-minimum-wage promoter, for example, Miller interjected that *he* favored a "$200,000 minimum wage"—quickly exposing the economic fallacy of his guest's argument.

Some viewers have expressed surprise at Miller's seriousness. "I don't want it to be irony-a-palooza like it's been in the past," he tells NewsMax's James Hirsen by way of explanation. "I think if I'm going to be on the show on a daily basis, talking about the issues of the world, I think people at least want to know that I did my homework, read a little, and I'm not up there doing a joke a minute and pissing on it," he adds.[27] With a quarter of young Americans now getting political news from "entertainment" programming like this, conservatives should be glad to have such a sharp, swift entertainer (mostly) on their side.

Not that Miller has become a partisan shill, as some liberals have charged. In fact, as critic Brendan Bernhard observed in *LA Weekly*, Miller is "considerably more interested in 'diversity' than some of his liberal counterparts"—selecting his guests in politically evenhanded fashion and usually treating them with great respect (with the notable exception of lefty critic Eric Alterman, openly mocked by the host in a tense segment for which he later apologized). Compare Miller's overall approach to, say, Charlie Rose's on PBS, and you'll quickly see who wins the fair-and-balanced prize.[28]

Why is cable and satellite TV entertainment less uniformly *Whoopi* than ABC, CBS, and NBC? Basically, for the same reason that cable news isn't as liberal-dominated as the networks: With long-pent-up market demand for programming that isn't knee-jerk liberal, cable's multiplicity of channels has given writers and producers who don't fit the elite-media mold the chance to meet that demand profitably.

Blogger Andrew Sullivan first came up with the term "South Park Republicans"—people who "believe we need a hard-ass foreign policy and are extremely skeptical of political correctness" but also are socially liberal on certain issues—to describe fans of this kind of cable-disseminated comedy.[29] Such South Park Republicanism is a real trend among younger Americans, he thinks. *South Park*'s typical viewer, it's worth noting, is an advertiser-ideal twenty-eight.

Talk to right-leaning college students, and it's clear that Sullivan may be on to something. Arizona State undergrad Eric Spratling says the definition fits him and his Republican pals perfectly. "The label is really about rejecting the image of conservatives as uptight squares—crusty old men or nerdy kids in blue blazers. We might have long hair, smoke cigarettes, get drunk on weekends, have sex before marriage, watch R-rated movies, cuss like sailors—and also happen to be conservative, or at least libertarian." Recent Stanford grad Craig Albrecht says most of his young Bush-supporter friends "absolutely cherish" *South Park*–style comedy "for its illumination of hypocrisy and stupidity in all spheres of life." It just so happens, he adds, "that most hypocrisy and stupidity take place within the liberal camp."[30]

Further supporting Sullivan's contention, Gavin McInnes, cofounder of Vice—a "punk-rock-capitalist" entertainment corporation that publishes the hipster bible *Vice* magazine, produces CDs and films, runs clothing stores, and claims (plausibly) to have been "deep inside the heads of eighteen-to-thirties for the past ten years"—spots "a new trend of young people tired of being lied to for the sake of the 'greater good.'" Especially on military matters, McInnes believes, many twenty-somethings are disgusted with the Left. The knee-jerk Left's days "are numbered," McInnes tells the *American Conservative*. "They are slowly but surely being replaced with a new breed of kid that isn't afraid to embrace conservatism."[31]

As we'll see in much greater detail in a later chapter, polling data and other evidence indicate that younger voters are indeed trending rightward—at one point supporting the Iraq War by a wider majority than their elders, viewing school vouchers favorably, and accepting greater restrictions on abortion, such as parental-notification laws (though more accepting of homosexuality than older voters). Together with the FOXification of cable news, this new attitude among the young, reflected in the hippest cable comedy, promises a more conservative future.

# The Blogosphere

**A**s CBS News can tell you, the rise of the Internet—something that really took off only twelve years ago, with the invention of the Netscape web browser—is the latest and perhaps most explosive change that is shaking liberal media dominance. It's hard to overstate the impact that news and opinion websites like the Drudge Report, FrontPage, NewsMax, and Dow Jones's OpinionJournal are having on politics and culture, as are current-event weblogs, or blogs—individual or group web diaries—like andrewsullivan.com, InstaPundit, Kausfiles, Power Line (whose central role in uncovering Rathergate we noted in our introduction), PoliPundit, and "The Corner" department of National Review Online, where the editors and writers argue, joke around, and call attention to articles elsewhere on the web. For simplicity's sake, let's refer to this whole universe of web-based discussion as the "blogosphere," though some apply that recently minted (post–September 11) term only to blogs proper.

While there are influential left-of-center sites—Joshua Micah Marshall's lively Talking Points Memo and liberal webzines Slate and Salon (both featuring blogs) come quickly to mind—the blogosphere currently leans right, albeit idiosyncratically, reflecting in part the hard-to-pigeonhole politics of some leading bloggers. Like talk radio and FOX News, the right-leaning sites fill a market void. "Many bloggers felt shut out by institutions that have adopted—explicitly or implicitly—a left-wing orthodoxy," says Erin O'Connor, whose blog, Critical Mass, exposes campus PC gobbledygook.[1]

The orthodox Left's blame-America-first response to September 11 gave a powerful rightward tilt to the blogosphere. "There were damned few noble responses to that cursed day from the 'progressive' part of the political spectrum," avers Los Angeles–based blogger and journalist Matt Welch, "so untold thousands of people just started blogs, in anger." Welch, who considers himself an "*Economist*-style" conservative liberal, was among them. "I was pushed into blogging on September 16, 2001, in direct response to reading five days' worth of outrageous bullshit in the media from people like Noam Chomsky and Robert Jensen."[2]

It's easy for frustrated citizens like Welch to get their ideas circulating on the Internet. Start-up and maintenance costs for a blog are small—less than $200 a year, thanks to easy-to-use technology invented by Pyra Labs in the late 1990s—and printing and mailing costs are of course nonexistent. Few blogs make a lot of money, though—or any— since some advertisers remain leery of the web, and no one seems willing to pay to read anything on it. Advertisers are starting to wake up to the web's power, however. The top sites can now charge anywhere from $300 to a couple of thousand bucks for a weeklong ad.

The absence of remuneration hasn't dampened the medium's scorching rate of growth. In 1999, there were fewer than one hundred blogs proper (web diaries, that is). Five years, later, the number has rocketed to more than four million and, according to some estimates, will soon reach ten million. "There are more bloggers *writing* . . . than people reading *USA Today* (whose circulation is 2.6 million)," web journalist Ed Driscoll points out.[3] Observes the *Dallas News*'s Rod Dreher,

"It makes every man and woman a publisher and is the most democratic form of journalism yet devised."[4] Many call the bloggers "citizen journalists."

Most blogs are indulgences, of zero interest to the general public and read only by family members and friends; most aren't political. But add the leading political blogs to the news and opinion websites that have proliferated since the late 1990s, and you really do have a brand-new media sphere—one that already is rivaling print, radio, and television for "mindshare," as *Wired* magazine calls it.

The Internet's most powerful effect has been to expand vastly the range of opinion—especially right-of-center opinion—at everyone's fingertips. "The Internet helps break up the traditional cultural gatekeepers' power to determine (a) what's important and (b) the range of acceptable opinion," says former *Reason* editor and libertarian blogger Virginia Postrel.[5] InstaPundit's Glenn Reynolds, a hawkish law professor at the University of Tennessee, agrees: "The main role of the Internet and blogosphere is to call the judgment of elites about what is news into question."[6]

The Drudge Report is a perfect case in point. Six years after the fedora-wearing, latter-day Walter Winchell Matt Drudge broke the Monica Lewinsky story, his news and gossip site has become an essential daily visit for political junkies, journalists, media types, and—with more than three *billion* visits to the site a year—seemingly anyone with an Internet connection. The site features newsworthy items investigated and written by Drudge, but it's primarily an editorial filter, linking to stories on other small and large news and opinion sites—a filter that crucially exhibits no bias against the Right. (Drudge, a registered Republican, calls himself "a pro-life conservative who doesn't want the government to tax me.")

Drudge enthusiast and cultural critic Camille Paglia observes that the site's constantly updated cornucopia of information, culled from a vast number of global sources and e-mailed tips from across the political spectrum, points up by contrast "the process of censorship that's going on, the filtering of the news by established news organizations."[7] Basically a two-man operation, Drudge now nets an estimated $70,000 a month, according to *Business 2.0*.[8]

RealClearPolitics, founded in 2000 by former Chicago options trader John McIntyre and friend Tom Bevan, a onetime ad executive, is an equally useful site for cutting through the liberal news fog. Every morning, RealClearPolitics links to the leading political editorials and news articles of the day, wherever they originate and whatever their political perspective. With your first few cups of coffee, you can read in one place—to take one typical day's samplings—a William Safire *New York Times* column, an Australian journalist eviscerating the United Nations for corruption, editorials from smaller-market daily papers like the *Rocky Mountain News* and the *Seattle Times*, top blogger commentaries, *U.S. News & World Report* wiseman Michael Barone analyzing America's voting dynamics, articles from the *Nation,* the *New Republic*, and the *Weekly Standard*, and McIntyre and Bevan's own informed musings.

And that's before you even get to the eye-poppingly comprehensive national and state polling data, transcripts of speeches, special interviews, think-tank reports, video feeds, and other raw information that the site gathers and organizes with luminous rationality. "The real value of what we do," Bevan says, "is to provide a daily political crib sheet— if you only have five minutes, you can still check in and get a quick snapshot of what is happening—as well as a kind of political almanac, in which you can spend as much time as you want reading and investigating issues and data."[9] RealClearPolitics was *the* place to go to keep abreast of the 2004 election, a fact to which several of the nation's leading political analysts attested. "It's one of the first things I get to every morning," said Barone. Similarly, Charlie Cook of the *National Journal* said: "Not a day goes by that I don't click on RealClearPolitics at least once, the presidential poll charts, graphs and moving averages are great." "RealClearPolitics is the first website I check every morning," declared *New York Times* columnist David Brooks. "It's an invaluable tool for anybody interesting in politics or public affairs." [10]

In a different register, Arts & Letters Daily, a site devoted to intellectual journalism, is similarly ecumenical in its links, posting articles from publications as diverse as *City Journal* on the right to the *New Left Review*. "Any contrarian, fresh view is a possibility for the site," says Arts & Letters Daily editor Denis Dutton, a philosophy professor at Canterbury University in New Zealand. "We certainly get complaints from all over the political spectrum, which I suppose is as it should be." Concurs managing editor Tran Huu Dung, "Both the right wing and left wing can see something they wouldn't normally read. That's the best thing about the page." [11] When Arts & Letters ran into financial trouble a couple of years back, both neoconservative elder Norman Podhoretz and *Nation* columnist and blogger Eric Alterman rushed to its defense. Going from 300 page views a day in 1998 to more than 88,000 a day in 2004, and with many left-leaning readers (including a large number of academics), it has introduced a whole new audience to serious conservative thought.

Though not quite in Drudge's league in readership, the top right-leaning sites, updated daily, have generated huge followings. Both InstaPundit and andrewsullivan.com (before Sullivan cut back on his blogging in early 2005) have attracted upward of two million visitors a month, making them two of the widest-read individual political blogs going (though traffic fluctuates radically). NewsMax's mix of take-no-prisoners conservative polemics, exposés of Hollywood idiocies, and news reports (including exclusives, such as the revelation of Bill Clinton's flubbed opportunity to nab Osama bin Laden in Sudan and Nancy Reagan's 2004 endorsement of George W. Bush for president) draws

more than two million readers a month, boasts half a million e-mail subscribers, and, unusual for the web, has generated an impressive revenue
stream. FrontPage, vigorously lambasting political correctness, the antiwar campaign, and other "progressive" follies, enjoys nearly as big an
audience. More than 1.4 million visitors landed on OpinionJournal in
March 2003, when the liberation of Iraq began, most to read editor
James Taranto's "Best of the Web Today," an incisive guide to and commentary on the day's top Internet stories. National Review Online
(NRO), featuring scores of substantive new articles daily, averages
slightly over one million visitors a month—and averaged over two million during the war. "More people read NRO than all the conservative
magazines combined," the site's editor at large, Jonah Goldberg, mar-
vels.[12] Feisty conservative forums FreeRepublic.com and Lucianne.
com, which give readers the opportunity to post and respond to news
items and articles—to become, in effect, minibloggers themselves—
have hundreds of thousands of monthly visitors. GOPUSA's web traffic (roughly half a million a month) is busy enough for founder Bobby
Eberle—a Houston engineer with no previous journalistic experience—
to land an exclusive interview with President Bush's political guru Karl
Rove. Hugh Hewitt's rapid-fire blog has drawn ten million visitors since
its beginning in early 2002.

The web's interconnectivity—the fact that bloggers and news/opinion
sites readily link to one another and comment on one another's postings,
forming a kind of twenty-first-century electronic agora—amplifies and
extends the influence of any site that catches the heavy hitters' attention. I can attest to this effect firsthand. On several occasions, online
versions of magazine essays I've written have been linked on a bunch of
heavily trafficked sites. The number of readers reached easily quintu-
pled the twenty thousand or so subscribers to the print publications.
Small wonder conservative print magazines like the *American Spectator*
and the *New Criterion* are using the web so extensively these days.

The large numbers of readers these sites attract isn't the only significant boost for the conservative cause; it's also *who* those readers are. Just as FOX News is pulling in a younger viewership who will reshape the politics of the future, so these conservative sites are proving particularly popular with younger people, 72 percent of whom are now online in the United States, according to an Online Publishers Association survey. "They think, 'If it's not on the web, it doesn't exist,'" says Goldberg. FrontPage's web traffic shoots up dramatically during the school year, as lots of college students log on. "Half of our online audience is under forty-five," says NewsMax chief and 1990s Clinton foe Chris Ruddy. "Younger readers are coming in."[13] *City Journal's* web readership skews significantly younger than its print subscribers, our in-house survey found. A Pew poll found that 20 percent of young adults now use the Internet as a top source for political information—and the percentage is rising every year.

Equally important, the blogosphere's citizen journalists draw the attention of many who work in the broader mediasphere (as we've already noted with regard to RealClearPolitics). Prominent political journalists and editors at ABC News (which has started its own inside-baseball political blog, The Note), CNN, the *Los Angeles Times*, *Newsweek*, the *New Yorker*, the *New York Times*, *Time*, *U.S. News & World Report*, and other major press and broadcast outlets have publicly stated that consulting political blogs and Internet sites has become a normal part of their workday. For CNN political analyst Jeff Greenfield, the blogosphere provides "access to a whole bunch of things that if you just read the *New York Times* and the *Washington Post* and watched broadcast networks and CNN you're not going to get."[14]

"Everyone who deals in media—and they're not all ideologues on the Left—is reading the Internet all the time," says FrontPage editor David Horowitz.[15] "Michael," who coauthors the 2blowhards culture/politics blog while working full-time for a major left-leaning national news organization (he uses a pseudonym because his bosses wouldn't like the blog's not-so-liberal opinions), reports, "I notice the younger people on staff in particular are aware of blogs—and that a lot of local newspapers seem to have people who stay on top of blogs, too."[16] The Internet's power, observes Mickey Kaus, the former *New Republic* writer whose Kausfiles blog (on Slate) has become indispensable reading for anyone interested in politics, "is due primarily to its influence over professional journalists, who then influence the public."[17] Judges Andrew Sullivan, "I think I have just as much ability to inject an idea or an argument into the national debate through my blog as I did through the *New Republic*," where he was the editor.[18]

Almost daily, stories that originate on the web make their way into print or onto TV or talk radio. FOX and Rush Limbaugh, for instance, often pick up stories from FrontPage and OpinionJournal—especially those about the antiwar Left. FOX News's Sean Hannity searches sites like Drudge and the Christian-right news site WorldNetDaily (another huge conservative web presence) for stories to cover on his radio and TV shows. "I'm addicted to being on the Internet," he tells me. "I'm literally on there hours and hours every day—reading everything, left-wing sites, conservative sites. That's where I do all my research."[19] Dennis Miller begins each morning by checking out Drudge. "He filters the kinds of news I'm interested in," says Miller.[20]

Phrases introduced in the blogosphere now "percolate out into the real world with amazing rapidity," InstaPundit's Glenn Reynolds notes.[21] For example, the day after the humor blog ScrappleFace coined the term "Axis of Weasel" to satirize the antiwar alliance of Jacques Chirac and Gerhard Schröder, the *New York Post* used it as a headline, talk radio, CNN, and FOX News repeated it, and it soon made its way into the French and German media.

Taking advantage of journalists' love of the Internet, right-of-center think tanks such as the American Enterprise Institute, the Heritage

Foundation, the Hudson Institute, and the Manhattan Institute now make all their policy research available online. Some state-based think tanks on the Right now have policy blogs too. A journalist or producer needing to get up to speed on welfare reform or crime prevention can find everything he needs from the conservative research camp with a mouse click or two. In the old pre-Internet days, if he even knew such studies existed, he would have had to wait days for them to arrive in the mail.

:: :: ::

The speed with which Internet sites can post new material is a key source of their influence. No sooner has the latest Paul Krugman *New York Times* column attacking the Bush administration appeared, for example, than the "Krugman Truth Squad"—a collective of conservative economic analysts—will post an article on NRO exposing the economist's myriad mistakes, distortions, and evasions. In 2003, the Truth Squad caught Krugman comparing the cost of Bush's tax cuts over *ten* years with the *one*-year wage boost associated with the new employment it would create, so as to make the tax reductions seem insanely large for the small benefit they'd bring—either a laughably ignorant mistake or a deliberate attempt to mislead in order to discredit Bush. The discomfiture web critics have caused Krugman has forced him to respond on his own website, offering various lame rationales for his errors and denouncing the Truth Squad's Donald Luskin as his "stalker-in-chief."

The timeliness of web publication also means that right from the start a wealth of conservative opinion is circulating about any new development—often before the *New York Times* and the *Washington Post* get a chance to weigh in. The blogosphere's "first-mover" advantage, note University of Chicago political scientist and blogger Daniel Drezner and George Washington University prof Henry Farrell, enables Internet writers to influence "political communication in the mainstream media through agenda setting and framing effects."[22] A blog or opinion site "can have an influence on elite opinion before the conventional wisdom among elites congeals," agrees Nick Schulz, editor of Tech Central Station, a site that covers technology and public policy.[23]

A case in point is the blogosphere "storm" or "swarm" (a ferocious burst of online argument, with site linking to site linking to site) that made a big issue out of the Democrats' unseemly transformation of Senator Paul Wellstone's funeral into a naked political rally, forcing the mainstream media to cover the story, which in turn created outrage that ultimately may have cost the Dems Wellstone's seat in the 2002 election. Blogosphere indignation over Republican senator Trent Lott's comments that seemed to praise segregation at onetime Dixiecrat Strom Thurmond's 100th birthday party, driven in part by NRO and other conservative sites keen to liberate modern conservatism from any vestige of racism and to make the GOP a champion of black advancement, shaped the mainstream media's coverage of that controversy, too—helping to push Lott from his perch as majority leader.

During the summer of 2004, mainstream media outlets initially ignored comedian Bill Cosby's politically incorrect remarks criticizing the failure of young blacks to learn proper English, which he saw as a major obstacle to African American success. But after education writer Joanne Jacobs and other bloggers raised a virtual tempest in support of Cosby's contention, the elite press had to report the story.

::          ::          ::

Debunking humbug—especially liberal humbug—is one of the web's most powerful political effects. Bloggers call it the Internet's "bullshit detector" role.

The *New York Times* has been the number-one target of the BS detectors—especially during the reign of deposed executive editor and liberal ideologue Howell Raines. "Only, say, five years ago, the editors of the *New York Times* had much more power than they have today," Andrew Sullivan points out. "They could spin stories with gentle liberal bias, and only a few eyes would roll."[24] If they made an egregious error, they could bury the correction later.

The Internet makes such bias and evasion harder—maybe impossible—to pull off. It was the blogosphere's army of cyber-ombudsmen that revealed Enron-bashing Krugman's former ties to Enron; showed how the *Times* twisted its polls to further its liberal agenda; exposed how the *Times* used its front page to place Henry Kissinger falsely in the anti–Iraq War camp, and then, as the war got under way, how the paper portrayed it as harshly as possible; demonstrated how columnist Maureen Dowd blatantly doctored a Bush quote to make the president look simple-minded; and (as mentioned earlier) helped discredit the election-eve report of missing weapons in Iraq.

The old-media world of the *Times* (and the network news) has always been a "high trust" environment, notes Glenn Reynolds. "You read something in the paper, or heard something from Dan Rather, and you figured it was probably true. You didn't ask to hear all the background, because it couldn't fit in a newspaper story, much less in the highly truncated TV-news format anyway, and because you assumed that they had done the necessary legwork."[25] The blogosphere explodes such "trust us" paternalism. "News becomes a conversation," explains *Entertainment Weekly* founder and blogger Jeff Jarvis. "It's not finished and fish wrap when it's printed. That's when the public finally gets to ask questions, contribute facts, and add new perspective."[26]

::     ::     ::

The blogosphere cost Raines his job—one of the first signs of its world-shaking might. When the story broke about the outrageous fabrications in the paper's pages of *Times* reporter and Raines favorite Jayson Blair, Andrew Sullivan (fired by Raines from his *New York Times Magazine* gig for his criticisms of his employer), Kaus, Drudge, blogger-reporter Seth Mnookin, and other web writers kept it alive, creating pressure for other media, including television, to cover it. Disgruntled *Times* staffers then began to leak damning information to Jim Romenesko's influential media-news site Poynter about the favoritism shown to Blair, presumably because he was African American (the *Times* had hired him through a minority recruitment program to make the paper "more diverse").

It turned out that Blair's supervisors at the *Times* had complained to higher-ups about the reporter's lousy and often unprofessional work habits and error-ridden reporting (the paper had to run fifty corrections on his stories over a three-and-a-half-year period). Yet *Times* executives chose to look the other way again and again and continued to fast-track Blair for promotions until the bloggers and other critics uncovered his lies. Kausfiles's "Howell Raines-O-Meter," gauging the probability of the editor's downfall, was up for barely a day or two when Raines stepped down. "The outcome would have been different without the Internet," Kaus rightly says.

The *Times*'s then ombudsman Daniel Okrent acknowledged the point: "We're not happy that blogs became the forum for our dirty linen, but somebody had to wash it and it got washed."[27] Raines's replacement as *Times* executive editor, Bill Keller, now keeps an eye on the blogosphere. "Sometimes I read something on a blog that makes me feel we screwed up," he told the *Washington Post*.[28]

The *Times* insisted that its quest for "diversity" had nothing to do with the fiasco, perfectly encapsulating the wishful-thinking-as-reality mind-set of the press when it comes to affirmative action. For the *Times*, to hire someone based on his race (as opposed to his qualifications) *couldn't* mean that he might not have the talent or temperament to do high-quality work, since that would mean that conservatives might have a point when it comes to the effects of affirmative action. Such a heretical thought has a hard time entering the liberal mind.

But ultimately the Blair affair was more final straw than primary cause of Raines's fall. Unremitting Internet-led criticism and mockery of the editor's front-page partisanship had already severely tarnished the *Times*'s reputation. It may take the *Times* quite a while to restore readers' trust: a Rasmussen poll shows that fewer than half of Americans believe that the paper reliably conveys the truth (while 72 percent find FOX News reliable).

Other liberal media giants have begun to take notice. In May 2003, the *Los Angeles Times*'s top editor, John Carroll, fired an e-mail to his troops warning that the paper was suffering from "the perception and the occasional reality that the *Times* is a liberal, 'politically correct' newspaper." In the new era of heightened web scrutiny, Carroll was arguing, you can't just dismiss conservative views but must take them seriously. Whether his paper has always managed to follow his advice is another question.

:: :: ::

Undercutting the liberal bias—the relentless pessimism and antiwar spin—of the mainstream media's coverage of the Iraq War and its aftermath are a growing number of pro-democracy Iraqi bloggers, whose on-the-scene reports describe a more hopeful, if far from ideal, reality. Making such specialized or "local" knowledge readily available, argue Drezner and Farrell (using F. A. Hayek's formulation), is another crucial service of the emerging blogosphere.

Twenty-four-year-old Baghdadi Zeyad's blog HealingIraq, for example, captured the true import of a December 2003 anti-terrorism rally in the Iraqi capital that the big media barely noticed. After moving through the surging crowd of 20,000 snapping pictures with a digital camera (paid for by prowar blogger Jeff Jarvis, who uploaded the photos onto the web), Zeyad discovered that the protest opposed more than just terrorism. "It was against Arab media, against the interference of neighboring countries, against dictatorships, against Wahhabism, against oppression, and of course against the Ba'ath and Saddam," Zeyad movingly wrote on his website. "At one point it struck me that our many differences as an Iraqi people meant nothing. Here we were all together shouting in different languages the same slogans, NO NO to terrorism, YES YES for peace."[29]

A second example. As revelations about prisoner abuse in Baghdad's Abu Ghraib prison commanded headlines in spring 2004, Iraqi blogger Ali posted the reflections of a physician friend who had treated inmates at the notorious jail. The upshot: While the abuse was a grave injustice, the doctor acknowledged, the publicizing of the abuse and the subsequent American crackdown on it showed how justice works in a free society. The Abu Ghraib analysis on Ali's then-site "should be required reading," said James S. Robbins on NRO.[30] Zeyad and Ali are only two of a budding community of Iraqi bloggers, many electronically dispatching from the Internet cafés that now dot block after Baghdad block—the very existence of which would have been unthinkable under Saddam. "The media is always taking a look at the bad stuff," Ali noted. "We want to show the good progress in Iraq."[31]

A lively Internet culture has blossomed in Iran, too, weakening the despotic mullahcracy's ability to control Iranian society, as a recent incident made clear. When the thuggish mullahs jailed blogger Sina Motallebi, fury roiled the blogosphere. Pro-democracy Iranian bloggers joined their Western sympathizers to express their anger at the injustice. As thousands and thousands of blog readers weighed in, the imprisonment became an international cause celebre, forcing the Iranian government to relent and release Motallebi. "They [the Iranian government] didn't expect the pressure from webloggers and foreign media in my case," Motallebi later related. "But the community of bloggers came together and helped me, and spread the news around the web, and became united."[32]

Farsi is now the fourth most widely used language on blogs worldwide, with one service provider hosting sixty thousand active Iranian blogs. "The weblogs allow young secular and religious Iranians to interact, partially taking the place of reformist newspapers that have been censored or shut down," Drezner and Farrell note. "Government efforts to impose filters on the Internet have been sporadic and only partially successful."[33]

The War on Terror has also marked the onset of "milblogs"—blogs pseudonymously written by active-duty military personal or reservists, who offer their own brand of specialized knowledge. The milblogs have fast made their presence felt. "Chief Wiggles" used his blog to run a toy drive for Iraqi kids; thousands of U.S. citizens chipped in. A marine blog reported that Al Jazeera was paying people to shoot at U.S. troops during Iraqi protests; military officials read the blog and had some Al Jazeera reporters arrested. More broadly, the milblogs give the public unmediated access to the views of the military, helping close some of the worrisome divide between martial and civilian outlooks that has opened in recent years. "Part of that problem was that the world of the warrior was increasingly remote from ordinary Americans who don't have much contact with the military," observes Hugh Hewitt, a leading theorist of the new media. "Milblogs are changing that condition."[34]

These new forms of Internet publishing will change warfare and diplomacy in the twenty-first century, predicts InstaPundit's Reynolds. "By undermining the power of the professional media organizations to present a negative image of war and to ignore dictators' crimes," he writes, "the new technology has made war against tyrants easier."[35] It's samizdat multiplied by orders of magnitude.

Not that the specialized knowledge on many right-side blogs and websites is solely about matters of war and peace. Sometimes, it's just knowing something in the liberal media is false because you were there. A good example came late in the summer of 2004. The Associated Press ran a disturbing item reporting that a crowd of Bush supporters in Wisconsin booed when the president told them to wish for Bill Clinton's speedy recovery from heart surgery, and that the president did nothing to stop them. The upshot: "You know those Republicans: They're haters one and all."

The story was bogus, insisted a little-known blogger named LisaS posting on the Right Voices site. "I was there at that particular Bush rally," she pointed out the next day. "I called my mom [who was at the rally] and asked her, 'Do you remember any booing?'" Mom didn't. LisaS asked her father and a friend, both at the rally too, and got the same answer: No booing. LisaS found an audio of the rally, proving the crowd didn't boo, and promptly posted it on Right Voices. LisaS then fired off e-mails alerting influential bloggers—and the AP—to the falsehood.[36] As the blogosphere began to discuss the story, the AP quietly scrubbed it of all references to booing, without issuing a retraction. Reynolds spells out the implications of such blogger interventions: "Things that used to be ignored, or spun, by the wholesalers of our news are now available retail. Cottage industry is competing with mass production, and with some success."[37]

Another example of the blogosphere's propagation of local knowledge: South Dakota blogs like Daschle v. Thune, Sibby Online, and South Dakota Politics have become counterweights to the local liberal newspaper, the *Sioux Falls Argus Leader*. Not only do they give national readers a better sense of the Byzantine complexities of the state's political scene, they also gave South Dakota voters a clearer picture of Democratic senator and minority leader Tom Daschle, who had the *Argus Leader* in his pocket. For years, Daschle had presented himself as a moderate to his conservative home state constituents, and the *Argus Leader* went along with the charade, neglecting to mention, for example, the senator's (literal) embrace of Michael Moore at the Washington opening of *Fahrenheit 9/11* and downplaying his partisan opposition to President Bush's policy agenda. The South Dakota blogs, their audiences building by the day, blew up this cozy relationship, contributing mightily to Daschle's loss to Republican John Thune in the 2004 election. "Agenda journalism isn't safe anymore," concludes Hewitt. "If you spin the facts, there are bloggers waiting to expose your partisanship. And the candidate you have been covering for."[38]

We can add countless other specialized sites. The Media Research Center website monitors press biases with remarkable thoroughness, as we saw earlier. The monomaniacal Moorelies logs Michael Moore's latest deceptions and distortions—a full-time job. Want to know what destructive craziness the trial lawyers are up to? Legal thinker Walter Olson records every jot and tittle on his constantly updated website Overlawyered. Along with being one of the first blogs to prove that the CBS Bush memos were forgeries, Little Green Footballs monitors the scarier corners of the Islamic press, as does the Middle East Media Research Institute site. And so on.

An additional gift the web has brought the Right is lots more humor. Like cable television, the blogosphere has incubated an anti-liberal comedic spirit—and nowhere more scathingly than on James Taranto's "Best of the Web" feature on OpinionJournal. "Even liberals, if they can get past his partisan views, can find him funny on occasion," a *New York* magazine profile of Taranto acknowledged.[39] Repetition (as *New York* noted) is a key weapon in Taranto's satiric arsenal. On OpinionJournal, John Kerry became, throughout 2003 and 2004, "the haughty, French-looking Massachusetts Democrat who by the way served in Vietnam"—capturing Kerry's out-of-touch aristocratic bearing, unceasingly issued reminders that he was a Vietnam vet, and thin-skinnedness. Corporate-bashing Krugman was invariably "former Enron adviser Paul Krugman."

Taranto also uses witty headings to mock the Left. "Moon Over Manhattan" introduced a riff on activists stripping naked to protest the Republican convention in New York. Under "Great Orators of the Democratic Party" ran the following quotes:

> "One man with courage makes a majority."—Andrew Jackson
> "The only thing we have to fear is fear itself."—Franklin Roosevelt
> "The buck stops here."—Harry Truman
> "Ask not what your country can do for you; ask what you can do for your country."—John F. Kennedy
> "For the first time in history, our generation may pass this country on to our children in worse shape than we were in fact handed it by our parents. And I believe that is an unacceptable principle worth fighting about, worth having an election about, worth changing the direction of this country for."—John Kerry

"Best of the Web" is argumentative as well as satirical, but Taranto thinks humor is particularly effective against today's philosophically bankrupt Left. "American liberals have run out of ideas, so instead they practice a politics of despair, rage, and sanctimony," he says. "They are deeply unserious people in extraordinarily serious times—and that makes them an irresistible target for anyone with a sense of humor."[40]

ScrappleFace, of "Axis of Weasels" fame, would agree with that insight. Started in 2002 by a young man named Scott Ott, the site consists of a seemingly inexhaustible stream of satirical news stories. Here's a witty short one from the 2004 Democratic convention, republished by the *Weekly Standard*. It pokes fun at John Kerry's well-deserved reputation for having been on all sides of all issues.

KERRY TO TELL UNDECIDED VOTERS: "I'M ONE OF YOU"

In a leaked excerpt of the nomination acceptance speech John
Forbes Kerry will deliver tonight at the Democratic convention,
the presidential candidate will tell undecided voters, "I'm one of
you."

Political strategists agree the message should resonate with the
independent and undecided Americans who Democrats and
Republicans alike view as their most valued constituency.

"If you don't know for whom you should vote, or how you stand
on the important issues of the day, " Mr. Kerry will say, "you have
a brother in John Kerry. I'm one of you."

The Democratic National Committee has already produced
thousands of red, white and blue placards that delegates will wave
during the speech, which read: "Undecided for Kerry."

Ott's mock newspaper headlines can also be quite amusing:

> "Kerry's Absence from Senate Not Reducing His Impact"
> "Dems Look Ahead: Whom to Hate in 2008"
> "Kerry: GOP Plans to Suppress Lawyer Turnout"
> "Bush Failed to Stop Al Qaeda During Clinton Years"
> "Bush Declares End of Major Campaign Operations"

ScrappleFace may be funny, but Ott insists his purpose is less humor
than getting ideas across. "My goal with ScrappleFace is not really parody, but clarity," he tells me. "It's not a humor site. I don't really care if
it's funny, and I rarely write just for laughs. I write the news the way it
ought to be, or the way it really is whether people acknowledge it or
not."[41] Whatever Ott is doing, it's working. The site attracts hundreds
of thousands of visitors a month, and its fake news items have been

written up in many top publications and read aloud on national radio
by Rush Limbaugh and other conservative talk-show hosts.

Then there's Chris Muir's blogosphere-born cartoon *Day by Day*—a
kind of conservative *Doonesbury* that has become a big hit among web
readers (200,000-plus a month) for its blend of wry humor and sharp
commentary. *Day by Day* revolves around a cast of four. Damon, a
twenty-five-year-old black software coder and entrepreneur, is the perhaps surprising voice of the Right. Sam is a forty-something mechani-
cal engineer, while Zed is an easygoing designer, "coasting through life,"
as Muir puts it. Jan, the fourth character, is a young marketer and raging lefty, with whom Damon regularly spars, as in this entry:

"My intention is to be the voice for the half of America that's had no
voice for the last twenty-five years in comics," Muir explains. "Not just
in politics, but in the man-woman dynamic, culture, trends—there's so
much to talk about." The talented cartoonist senses a "seismic" gener-
ational shift that is increasing the demand for his kind of politically
incorrect humor. In Muir's view, young people "are tired of the non-
sensical groupthink of aging boomers."

Thanks to the blogosphere, Muir can cut through the PC filter of
mainstream syndicates and editors. "Blogs are becoming the 'buzz' of
society, a platform where the culture sorts itself out," he maintains.
"Strictly word-of-blog accounts for *Day by Day*'s growing audience."[42]
Relying on the Internet's instantaneousness, Muir can do his cartoons

just one hour before posting them, which means that topicality is never the problem that it can be for syndicated cartoonists, who usually need to finish their daily entries weeks before publication.

::     ::     ::

Despite Al Gore's much-derided claim that he fathered the Internet, liberals have tended to distrust the wild and unregulated blogosphere. The *Boston Globe*'s Alex Beam gives an oft-heard liberal response: "Welcome to Blogistan, the Internet-based journalistic medium where no thought goes unpublished, no long-out-of-print book goes unhawked, and no fellow 'blogger,' no matter how outré, goes unpraised."[43] Veteran *Washington Post* reporter David Broder even blames the shoddy journalistic ethics evident in the mainstream media of late on the bloggers! "When the Internet opened the door to scores of 'journalists' who had no allegiance at all to the skeptical and self-disciplined ethic of professional news gathering, the bars were already down in many old-line media organizations," he wrote with disgust. "This is how it happened that old pros such as Dan Rather and former *New York Times* editor Howell Raines got caught up in this fevered atmosphere and let their standards slip."[44] And of course, as we saw in our introduction, you had the former executive vice president of CBS News (and now head of CNN's news group), Jonathan Klein, dismissing the blogger "sitting in his living room in his pajamas writing." The pajama people get the editor of the *Argus Leader* spitting bile: "True believers of one

stripe or another, no longer content to merely bore spouses and neigh-
bors with their nutty opinions, can now spew forth on their own
blogs. . . . If Hitler were alive today, he'd have his own blog."[45] In other
words: How dare the peasants!

Such elitist contempt toward Internet publishing is diminishing on
the Left these days, though, especially after Howard Dean (or better,
his tech-savvy campaign boss Joe Trippi) showed during the Democratic presidential primaries just how much money and interest a left-wing
candidate could raise via the web. Bloggers also received press passes
to the 2004 Democratic and Republican conventions—a historic first.

Nonetheless, liberal unease about the Internet remains. In his 2001
book *Republic.com*, legal theorist Cass Sunstein argued that the increasing influence of the web's political sites could lead to a kind of cyber-
balkanization (I'm indebted here to Drezner and Farrell's excellent
discussion of this problem). "New technologies, emphatically including
the Internet, are dramatically increasing people's ability to hear echoes
of their own voices and to wall themselves off from others," Sunstein
noted. "In a system in which each person can 'customize' his own communications universe, there is a risk that people will make choices that
generate too little information, at least to the extent that individual
choices are not made with reference to their social benefits."[46] In an
article headlined "People Getting News They Want—Not the News
They Need," the *Los Angeles Times*'s David Shaw struck a similar note,
complaining about the "intellectually lazy" people who now get their
news from the Internet, where their views find "reinforcement and val-
idation," instead of seeking out the unbiased reporting of the traditional
news media. "[W]hat Matt Drudge calls news is very different from
what, say, Walter Cronkite called news," Shaw opined sourly.

Worries about such virtual cocooning may be exactly contrary to the
truth. Blogger and Yale law prof Jack Balkin gives one explanation why.
"[Most] bloggers who write about political subjects cannot avoid

addressing (and, more importantly, linking to) arguments made by people with different views," he points out. "The reason is that much of the blogosphere is devoted to criticizing what other people have to say. It's hard to argue with what the folks at National Review Online or Salon are saying unless you go read their articles, and, in writing a post about them, you will almost always either quote or link to the article or both."[47] NRO and the New Republic website have occasionally run an "Opinion Dual" in which writers from each camp debate major issues, with their back-and-forth appearing simultaneously on both sites.

At *City Journal*, the Internet has brought us numerous new readers who don't share our politics. Before we started posting our articles on the web, we'd get the occasional letter from an angry liberal who'd come across us in a library or from a newspaper mention or excerpt. Now that we've entered the blogosphere era, we get bombarded with e-letters from the Left, especially when an ecumenical site like Arts & Letters Daily or RealClearPolitics links to us. Most of the left-wing letter writers curse us out. Others make thoughtful criticisms. And a few say, "Wow, you've changed my mind." How is that cyber-balkanization? Isn't it just democratic debate in action?

::          ::          ::

But that debate for "mindshare" is what many on the Left—the illiberal liberals—really object to, as we've seen. Liberals yearn for the good old days when everybody who didn't read *National Review* had to get his news and analysis from "unbiased" old-media sources like CBS and the *New York Times* and conservative arguments could be dismissed with an insult or, better still, simply ignored.

None of this is to say that the blogosphere is without drawbacks. Lots of what circulates in the blogosphere is unfounded gossip, misinformed venting, or just plain trivial. Most blogs show what happens when writers can bypass editors. Yet at its best, Matt Welch rightly argues, the blogosphere "is among the most exciting new trends the [journalism] profession has seen in a while."[48] For John Fund, the best blogs and news and opinion sites are "building a shadow media infrastructure that will become a significant component of the media in the twenty-first century."[49]

As this chapter has shown, it's a new universe that the Right has proved it can compete in, and even win in. The same is increasingly true of the old medium of book publishing, as we will see in the next chapter.

# Chapter Seven

# The Conservative Book Publishing Revolution

Conservative authors long had trouble getting their books released by major publishing houses, with only Regnery Publishing, the Free Press, and Basic Books regularly releasing conservative titles. But following editorial changes during the 1990s, Basic and the Free Press published far fewer conservative leaning titles, leaving Regnery pretty much alone in the field.

No more. Nowadays, publishers are falling all over themselves to bring conservative books to a mainstream audience. "Between now and December," *Publishers Weekly* wrote in July 2003, noticing the new trend for the first time, "scores of books on conservative topics will be published by houses large and small—the most ever produced in a single season."[1] Rarely a week now goes by without a new conservative book hitting the bestseller lists. From 2000 through the summer of 2004, eighteen of the thirty bestselling political books were conservative.

Make no mistake: This development is hugely significant. Books are one of the essential ways American politics and culture sort themselves out. "There is nothing like a book," social thinker Michael Novak rightly notes. "Held in hand. Underlined. Kept on shelf nearby. Remembered for years. People *expect* to be moved by books, to learn, to be changed."

Jed Donahue, a young New York editor at Random House, enthusiastically affirms the point. "Nothing can match books for in-depth arguments and analyses," he says. In Dick Morris's view, the spike in demand for political books is fed by the desire for rich analysis that only books can provide. "The depth of voter knowledge and interest and intensity does not match the superficiality of thirty-second ads," Morris observes. "So there is a desire to go deeper, which books gratify."[2]

By influencing both elite and popular opinion, books can transform policy and culture in deep and abiding ways. Think of how Michael Harrington's *The Other America*, published in 1962, triggered the war on poverty or how Charles Murray's 1984 book *Losing Ground* planted the seeds of welfare reform (as President Bill Clinton acknowledged twenty-two years later when he signed the bill ending the federal welfare entitlement) or how Myron Magnet's *The Dream and the Nightmare* influenced President Bush's "compassionate conservatism" approach in the 2000 election. Books matter.

Consumer demand has prompted two superpower publishers to set up new imprints to compete with Regnery in mass-market right-leaning books: Random House's Crown Forum (where Donahue works), launched in late 2003, and Sentinel, a Penguin imprint that debuted in August 2004. Between them, the new imprints will publish and promote upward of thirty books a year.

Timely conservative polemics make up a portion of the two imprints' lists. Among Crown Forum's early releases, for example, are James Hirsen's *Tales from the Left Coast*, a fierce attack on Hollywood liberals co-published with NewsMax, and Ann Coulter's *Treason* and *How to Talk to a Liberal (If You Must)*, while Sentinel's freshman list announced journalist Mona Charen's *Do-Gooders: How Liberals Hurt Those They Claim to Help (And the Rest of Us)* and Richard Chesnoff's *The Arrogance of the French: Why They Can't Stand Us—and Why the Feeling Is Mutual*.

But the new imprints are also publishing broader works of intellectual history and social analysis, such as historian Thomas DiLorenzo's *How Capitalism Saved America* (Crown Forum) and social critic Mary Eberstadt's *Home-Alone America: The Hidden Toll of Day Care, Behavioral Drugs, and Other Parent Substitutes* (Sentinel). Steve Ross, Crown Forum's publisher, describes his titles as targeting "up-market" readers, "affluent, sophisticated, very aware of current events and intellectually hungry."[3] Sentinel editor Bernadette Malone says much the same, adding that the Penguin line will also publish conservative works of humor and memoirs.

These presses will thrive, early evidence suggests. In its first several months, Crown Forum rocketed four books onto the *New York Times* bestseller list, with Coulter's *Treason* hitting 550,000 copies in print. Sentinel's early releases have sold briskly, with Ronald Kessler's *A Matter of Character: Inside the White House of George W. Bush* debuting at number twelve on *Publishers Weekly's* bestseller list in late August 2004.

::        ::        ::

Highbrow mid-list books now pour forth monthly from several other Right-friendly presses. Peter Collier's Encounter Books took flight in 2000, specializing in serious works of history, culture, and political analysis aimed at both conservatives and open-minded liberals. "I know. . . the desire readers have for books that are worth their while, books that leave them subtly changed—more intelligent and more alive than they were before they read them," Collier told a reporter a few years ago, explaining why he thought Encounter could make a difference in the nation's intellectual life.[4] Encounter has published such worldview-altering works as Roger Kimball's demolition of contemporary art criticism, *The Rape of the Masters*; Jean-François Revel's *Anti-Americanism*, one of the sharpest books yet written on the topic; and Sol Stern's *Breaking Free*, a memoir about the struggle for school choice that won a 2004 Independent Publishers Association award for best education book.

After just a few years in business, Encounter Books is selling $3 million worth of books a year, Collier says.[5] Several Encounter titles have sold in the 35,000 range, and a Bill Kristol–edited volume laying out the reasons for the war in Iraq has sold over 60,000 copies.

ISI Books—the newly active book arm of the Intercollegiate Studies Institute, the venerable conservative group that defends "the American ideal of ordered liberty" on university campuses—is enjoying similar success with its expanding list of brainy titles. Releasing high-minded works by leading intellectuals of the Right—constitutional scholar Robert P. George's *The Clash of Orthodoxies* and British philosopher Roger Scruton's *The West and the Rest: Globalization and the Terrorist Threat* are two notable examples—the founder of the imprint, Jeff Nelson, says he wants to "get beyond and beneath political squabbling on the surface." Nelson counts among his heroes legendary publisher Henry Regnery. "Political conservatism depends on traditional intellectual conservatism. Issues may change on the surface, but core ideas need to be continually redefined and probed," Nelson believes. "As conservatism becomes more politicized, a group that upholds core principles and philosophy is more vital."[6] Adds ISI Books editor in chief Jeremy Beer, "We are, or at least try to be, the most intellectual of conservative book publishers—without being inaccessible or of interest solely to academics."[7]

ISI Books's wonderful "student guides," written by first-rate scholars such as John Lukacs (on history) and Harvey Mansfield (on political philosophy), exemplify this intention perfectly, showing undergraduates how to educate themselves in the riches of the Western tradition. Students are unlikely to get such an education from today's professoriate, which tends to despise Western culture as patriarchical, racist, exploitative, or whatever the latest trendy grievance happens to be. Hundreds of thousands of the guides are now in print. (We'll come back to ISI's work on campus in the next chapter.)

Recognizing the emergent market for conservative titles, ISI Books recently branched out with two new series. "Crosscurrents" commissions new translations of classic and contemporary conservative thought (I serve on an advisory panel for the series). Its first titles include Aleksandr Solzhenitsyn's *Russia in Collapse*, the Nobel Prize–winner's first book in English in nearly a decade, and an anthology of eighteenth- and nineteenth-century French counter-Enlightenment thought. "Foundations" publishes children's books that uphold traditional values. *Everyday Graces: A Child's Book of Good Manners*, an anthology edited by Karen Santorum, wife of Republican senator from Pennsylvania Rick Santorum, and *The National Review Treasury of Classic Children's Literature*, selected by William F. Buckley, kicked off the series.

ISI Books titles sell on average anywhere between 7,000 and 15,000 copies, with the Santorum volume exceeding 25,000 in sales. Revenues for ISI Books have quadrupled over the past few years, to nearly $1 million a year—an impressive rate of growth in today's publishing industry.

Ivan R. Dee, out of Chicago, has also been releasing a steady flow of right-of-center scholarly titles: new editions of past classics such as Gertrude Himmelfarb's profiles of *Victorian Minds* and Elie Kedourie's study of the modern Middle East, *The Chatham House Version and Other Middle-Eastern Studies*, as well as highly praised collections of recent essays from *City Journal* and the *New Criterion*. The Liberty Fund, in turn, has built a thick catalogue of new editions of conservative and libertarian standards, ranging from David Hume's six-volume *History of England* and Lord Acton's *Lectures on the French Revolution* to Forrest McDonald's *E Pluribus Unum* and Bertrand de Jouvenel's *On Power*. (Liberty Fund also organizes numerous conferences devoted to great books.) Transaction Publishers, under the leadership of sociologist

Irving Louis Horowitz, makes newly available great works of social science and humanistic studies by such stalwarts of the Right as Robert
Nisbet and Raymond Aron. Thanks to the efforts of these publishers,
among others, there are fewer and fewer important conservative works
currently out of print.

Nor is that all. WorldNetDaily has rolled out its own conservative
book line, releasing, among other hits, hard-right firebrand Michael
Savage's what's-wrong-with-America blast *Savage Nation* (which topped
the *New York Times*'s bestseller list) and Richard Poe's *Hillary's Secret
War*, narrating how web publications like Lucianne.com, FreeRepub-
lic.com, NewsMax, and WorldNetDaily kept tabs on Clinton misdeeds
during the 1990s. The Christian publisher Thomas Nelson has put out
a series of hot-selling books by Hugh Hewitt. Yale University Press,
Lexington Books, Ignatius Press, and Spence Books all regularly release
conservative titles. Some other major publishers now habitually acquire
books that flout liberal orthodoxy—ReganBooks, Michael Moore's publisher, for instance, has put out David T. Hardy and Jason Clarke's sar-
castic smash *Michael Moore Is a Big Fat Stupid White Man* and several
other right-leaning bestsellers.

And all this is on top of the extraordinary number of serious books
on the American founding fathers to appear over the last few years—
conservative not in an immediately political sense, perhaps, but recognizing the greatness of figures such as John Adams, Alexander
Hamilton, and other American giants in ways sure to infuriate the left-
wing academy, which scorns them as White Male Oppressors.

Even tiny presses are getting in on the act. The two-year-old ENC
Press (Emperor's New Clothes) publishes literary fiction with a con-
servative or a *South Park* anti-PC bent, targeting "the emerging inde-
pendent-thinker counterculture," says founder and publishing veteran
Olga Gardner Galvin.[8] Its catalogue boasts a new translation of
Yevgheniy Zamyatin's 1920 book *We*, the anti-totalitarian book that

helped inspire *1984*, *Brave New World*, *Anthem*, and the whole literary genre of dystopia.

This burgeoning right-wing book market has led corporate giant Bookspan, which runs the Book-of-the-Month Club, to start a new conservative book club, American Compass, headed by former *National Review* literary editor Brad Miner. "Increasingly, readers are telling us they want to read books with a conservative point of view," explained Bookspan CEO Markus Wilhelm in announcing the venture, which will compete with the longer-standing Conservative Book Club.[9] Wilhelm has tasked Miner with acquiring conservative titles for the company's other book clubs as well.

American Compass has exploded out of the gate, enrolling two thousand members in its first several months. Better still, members are gobbling up club offerings. "In terms of sales-per-catalogue, which is an important determiner of the health of long-term viability of American Compass, we're about as high as any club has ever been," Miner happily points out.[10]

::     ::     ::

It's no exaggeration to describe this surge of conservative publishing as a paradigm shift. "It would have been unthinkable ten years ago that mainstream publishers would embrace this trend," acknowledges Doubleday editor and author Adam Bellow, who got his start in editing in 1988 at the Free Press, where he and his boss, the late Erwin Glikes, encountered "a tremendous amount of marketplace and institutional resistance" in pushing conservative titles.[11] "There was no conspiracy," avers Crown Forum publisher Ross. "We were culturally isolated on this island of Manhattan, and people tend to publish to people of like mind."[12]

For many in New York publishing, hostility to the Right was indeed instinct. Back in the early 1990s, when editor Judith Regan, then with Pocket Books, acquired Rush Limbaugh's first book, *The Way Things*

*Ought to Be*, a collection of the talk-show host's observations deftly put together by the *Wall Street Journal*'s John Fund, she mortified her colleagues, who viewed Limbaugh as a nutcase. "The editorial director said, 'Judith has reached a new low,' and people booed," she later recalled. "People left nasty notes around the office and even in the bathroom."[13] The collection sold upward of three million copies in a matter of months, becoming one of the bestselling nonfiction books in American history—an early sign of how successful conservative titles could be. (Even earlier, in 1960, Barry Goldwater's *Conscience of a Conservative* sold 100,000 copies. The publisher? A tiny Kentucky-based outfit called Victor Publishing.)

Ross believes that the attacks of September 11 shook up the publishing world and made it less reflexively liberal. And in fact, many new conservative titles concern the War on Terror. But what really overcame the big New York publishers' liberal prejudices was the oodles of money Washington-based Regnery was making. "We've had a string of bestsellers that is probably unmatched in publishing," Regnery president Marji Ross observes. "We publish twenty to twenty-five titles a year, and we've had sixteen books on the *New York Times* bestseller list over the last four years—including Bernard Goldberg's *Bias*, which spent seven weeks at number one."[14] Adds Bernadette Malone, the former Regnery editor heading up Penguin's Sentinel imprint, "The success of Regnery's books woke up the industry: 'Hello? There's 50 percent of the population that we're underserving, even ignoring. We have an opportunity to talk to these people, figure out what interests them, and put out professional-quality books on topics that haven't been sufficiently explored.'"[15] Bellow puts it more bluntly: "Business rationality has trumped ideological aversion. And that's capitalism."[16]

With the book industry at last beginning to wake from its dogmatic liberalism, "the sky may be the limit for conservative books," says American Compass's Miner. "We don't yet know the upper extent to which conservative books can be published in the U.S. Every time a new conservative imprint comes along, it manages to create bestsellers," he points out. Miner believes American Compass can grow its membership into the hundreds of thousands.

::       ::       ::

There's another key reason that conservative books are selling: the emergence of conservative talk radio, cable TV, and the Internet. This "right-wing media circuit," as *Publishers Weekly* describes it, reaches millions of potential readers and thus makes the traditional gatekeepers of ideas—above all, the *New York Times Book Review* and *The New York Review of Books*, publications that rarely deign to review conservative books, and more rarely still review them favorably—increasingly irrelevant in winning an audience for a book. "This is the most exiting dynamic to develop in the last twenty years," marveled conservative public relations guru Craig Shirley in an interview. "We did Wayne LaPierre's book, *Guns, Crime and Freedom*, but we could never get the *Washington Post*, the *New York Times*, the *Boston Globe* or the *L.A. Times* to review it," Shirley elaborated. "But talk radio paid attention, and one of the reasons it became a bestseller is that we booked Wayne on something like 270 radio talk shows over a six-month period."[17]

Encounter Books publisher Peter Collier shares Shirley's enthusiasm for the marketing power of the new media. Instead of worrying about high-profile reviews in the media mainstream—"I've had God knows how many books published by now, and maybe three reviews in the *New York Times Book Review*," says Collier, laughing—Encounter sells books by getting its authors discussed on the Internet and interviewed on talk radio, FOX News, and C-SPAN's ideologically neutral book programs. "A Q & A on NRO sells books very, very well," Collier explains. "It's comparable to a major newspaper review."[18] A bold Drudge Report headline will move far more copies than even good newspaper reviews, claims Regnery's Marji Ross. A book discussed on andrewsullivan.com will briefly blast up the Amazon.com bestseller list—even hitting the top five. NewsMax or WorldNetDaily can by themselves practically lift a book onto the national bestseller lists. A mention from a talk-radio heavyweight like Rush Limbaugh, Laura Ingraham, or Dr. Laura Schlessinger or a chat on FOX News can also drive up an author's sales dramatically.

FOX News's hosts and contributors, taking advantage of the station's mushrooming audience, have become a cottage book industry all by themselves. Bill O'Reilly, Sean Hannity, Dick Morris, Neal Cavuto, and John Gibson have all come out with conservative-themed tomes in recent months, which have sold bundles despite being all but ignored by the elite press. "The thing about the FOX books," says Miner, "is that their authors have a loyal audience watching them and hanging onto their every word, week after week. That builds up a sense of authority, and those guys have it." As O'Reilly remarked to Laura Ingraham, "We don't need them to review our books."[19]

Amazon is another godsend to conservatives, since the Internet giant betrays no ideological bias in selling books. Nor do big chain booksellers like Wal-Mart, Costco, and Barnes & Noble, often accounting for more than 40 percent of the sales of a bestseller. Targeting small towns and suburbs—and red-state America in general—Wal-Mart won't sell anything that might offend its culturally conservative shoppers, so you won't find any raunchy CDs or books or magazines with offensive covers. That in turn has forced publishers and entertainers to tone down their products in order to reach the company's huge customer base. Wal-Mart has thus become "a powerful force for cultural conservatism," notes one Christian writer—an "example of the economic marketplace correcting bad culture."[20]

In these retailers, Hugh Hewitt's forceful conservative books pile up right next to Michael Moore's latest attack on the Right. "The rise of

Amazon and the chain stores has been tremendously liberating for conservatives, because these stores are very much product-oriented businesses," observes FrontPage editor David Horowitz. "The independent bookstores are all controlled by leftists, and they're totalitarians—they will not display conservative books, or if they do, they'll hide them in the back."[21] Says Marji Ross, "We have experienced our books being buried or kept in the back room when a store manager or owner opposed their message."

Some resentful liberal clerks at the big chains also seem comfortable with such tactics, even if corporate management isn't. After Swift Boat veteran John O'Neill's explosive anti-Kerry book *Unfit for Command* hit the bestseller list in the summer of 2004, customers were initially having a hard time finding the book at Barnes & Noble and Borders, leading to accusations that the chains were censoring it. The main reason the books were scarce, it turned out, was that online websites such as the Drudge Report began talking about the book before it was even printed, but anyone reading posts on the Borders employee union website could be forgiven for thinking a darker force was afoot. "We're 'finding' [note those quotation marks] that most of the few copies we're getting are damaged and need to be sent back," one clerk sarcastically wrote. "So sad. Too bad, Bushies! Regnery needs to be more careful. I'm hearing from people at two other stores that this seems to be common." In a later post, the clerk became even blunter. "You guys don't actually HAVE to sell the thing," he told his fellow unionists. "Just 'carelessly' hide the boxes, 'accidentally' drop them off pallets, 'forget' to stock the ones you have, then suggest a nice Al Franken or Michael Moore as a substitute. . . . I don't care if these Neanderthals in fancy suits get mad at me. They aren't regular customers anyway. Other than 'Left Behind' books, they don't read. Anything you can do to make them feel unwelcome is only fair." Another Borders employee added, "I wish [conservative book buyers] really knew how little respect I have for them."[22]

The president of Borders International stores, Vin Altruda, quickly wrote *National Review* to reassure conservatives that such employee sabotage "would not be tolerated under any circumstances." "Borders is absolutely apolitical," Altruda emphasized. "We take no stance whatsoever and for more than thirty years have remained committed to our customers' right to choose what to read and what to buy." Further, he wrote, "we take great measures to communicate this to our employees and to emphasize the importance of not expressing political viewpoints while at work in our stores. In fact, this political season, I have personally communicated strongly to all employees that political expression is not appropriate in the workplace."[23]

Yet even the lefty independents are starting to acknowledge the existence of conservative books. Consider a midtown Manhattan independent bookstore that I frequent, the kind of place that stacks *Bushisms* and anti-Republican playing cards at the checkout counter. Several years ago, it carried few of the (fewer number of) top right-of-center titles. Now, though, the store does stock most top conservative books. The relative glasnost testifies to the free market's might. When a conservative book propelled by Drudge, talk radio, FOX, and sales at Amazon and the big chains becomes a national bestseller, the independents usually have to carry it if they want to stay in business. I recently overheard a clerk at the independent bookstore whining, "I wish we didn't carry Ann Coulter's stuff. I hate her so much. But people always ask for her, so we gotta, I guess." The store managers still do their petty best to fight the Right, placing conservative hits on lower shelves and prominently displaying just about every mass-market liberal book existent. But the times, they are a'changin'.

Amazon's Customer Reviews feature—where readers can post their opinions on books they've read and rate them—has helped diminish the authority of elite cultural guardians by creating a truly democratic marketplace of ideas. "I don't think there's ever been a similar review medium—a really broad-based consumers' guide for culture," says 2blowhards blogger "Michael." "I've read some stuff on Amazon that's been as good as anything I've read in the real press."[24]

Amazon readers' obsessive lists, popping up on your screen when you call up a particular book, can also be terrifically informative. Punch in, say, "Robert Bork," and you straight away see three lists: "Federalist Society Reading List," by "Dausha"; "Books to Annoy Your Neighborhood Liberal," by "Basfawlty, American"; and "Conservative Roots," by "kspeck 3." Each proffers recommendations of other conservative books, accompanied by brief comments by the list makers. Pretty soon, you've got dozens of right-of-center titles to choose from, from William F. Buckley's classic first book *God and Man at Yale* to Thomas Sowell's *The Vision of the Anointed: Self-Congratulation as a Basis for Social Policy*. Amazon, it turns out, is an amazing educational tool.

::　　::　　::

Liberals—predictably—grouse that all these right-wing books are a danger to society. Their "bile-spewing" authors "have limited background expertise and a great flair for adding fuel to hot issues," claims Norman Provizer, a *Rocky Mountain News* columnist.[25] "The harm is if people start thinking these lightweights are providing heavyweight answers." Ellen Heltzel, one of the "Book Babes" whose column runs on the Poynter website, laments the existence of the new conservative imprints, since it means the "strident voices" of the Right now have "a larger platform from which to spiel their predictable line." The conservative books serve "to polarize more than inform," she adds.[26]

Sour grapes, I'd say. How were Americans better informed in the days when conservatives had difficulty finding publishers and wide readership? Would the nation's political and cultural life be healthier if, say, the sixty or so tomes bashing President Bush that inundated bookstores in the run-up to the 2004 presidential election—blaring titles like *Bushwhacked*, *The Bush-Hater's Handbook*, *The I Hate George W. Bush Reader*, *The Lies of George W. Bush*, and *Worse Than Watergate*—had not been countered to some degree by the smaller number of pro-Bush bestsellers like Kessler's *A Matter of Character* or anti-Kerry smashes like John O'Neill's *Unfit for Command* (with nearly half a million sold as of January 2005)?

Liberals might think so: Many blamed the impact of O'Neill's *Unfit* for Kerry's defeat. But the alternative to "polarization" that the Left really yearns for is a world without conservative books—and for that matter, without NRO, Dennis Miller, FOX News, Rush Limbaugh, and, well, conservatives period. Happily, that yearning will remain unsatisfied, even if the Right is (for now) still outnumbered in the mediasphere.

What's more, the surprisingly conservative political and cultural views of American youth, considered in the next chapter, mean that there probably will be an even bigger audience for conservative books—for right-of-center argument in general—in the years to come. "These are values, not the superficial stuff," Miner notes. "As these people age, they're probably going to move along that base to an even more conservative outlook."

# Chapter Eight

# Campus Conservatives Rising

**T**hroughout 2003 and into 2004, a surge of protests roiled American campuses. You probably think the kids were agitating against war in Iraq, right? Well, no: students at UCLA, the University of New Mexico, the University of Michigan, and many other schools were sponsoring bake sales to protest . . . affirmative action. For white students and faculty, a cookie cost (depending on the school) $1; blacks and Hispanics could buy one for a lot less. The principle, the protesters observed, was the same as that governing university admission practices: rewarding people differently based on race. Indignant school officials charged the bake sale organizers with "creating a hostile climate" for minority students, oblivious to the incoherence of their position. On what grounds could they favor race preferences in one area (admissions) and condemn them in the other (selling cookies) as racist? Several schools banned the sales on flimsy pretexts such as the organizers' lack of school food permits.

The protests shocked the mainstream press, but to close observers of America's college scene lately, they came as no surprise. For decades, conservative critics have bemoaned academe's monolithically liberal culture. Parents, critics note, spend fortunes to send their kids to top colleges and then watch helplessly as the schools cram them with a diet of politically correct leftism often wholly opposed to Mom and Dad's own values.

But the Left's long dominion over the university—the last place on Earth the Left's power would break up, conservatives believed, just after the elite media—is showing its first signs of weakening. The change isn't coming from the schools' faculty lounges and administrative offices, of course. It's coming from self-organizing right-of-center students and several innovative outside groups working to bypass academia's elite gatekeepers.

There've always been conservative students on campus: More than a half-century has passed since a just-graduated William F. Buckley published *God and Man at Yale*, lamenting his alma mater's secularism and launching the author on his now-legendary career. Yet never has the Right flourished among college kids as it does today.

The number of College Republicans is a good marker. Six years ago, the organization claimed just over four hundred campus chapters. Now that the number has almost tripled, to 1,148, with 120,000-plus members (compared with the College Democrats' 900 or so chapters and 100,000 members). What's more, the College Republicans are thriving on elite campuses. "We've doubled in size over the last few years, to more than four hundred students," Evan Baehr, a square-jawed future pol heading the Princeton chapter, informs me.[1] The numbers of University of Pennsylvania College Republicans have also rocketed upward, says chapter president Stephanie Steward. "When I started a couple of years ago," she explains, "we had roughly twenty-five members, only about four of them active. Today [late 2004], we have seven hundred members on our listserve, we had over three hundred people at our first meeting this year, and have about seventy active members who regularly attend events." Same story at Harvard. These young

Republican activists, trudging into battleground states in 2004 get-out-the-vote efforts, helped George W. Bush win.

Other conservative organizations, ranging from gun clubs (Harvard's, founded a few years ago, has more than one hundred students blasting away) to impudent student newspapers and magazines, are budding at schools everywhere—even at Berkeley, crucible of the 1960s student Left. The Leadership Institute, a nonprofit that trains future right-of-center leaders, helps organize conservative clubs on campus and saw the number double in 2004—from 216 to over 400. And right-of-center authors invited by student clubs to speak on campus are drawing large and approving crowds. "At many schools, those speeches have become the biggest events of the semester," *Time* reports. A student-sponsored lecture at Duke in 2003 by conservative author and former Comedy Central host Ben Stein, for instance, attracted 1,500 listeners, 200 over capacity, and "a bigger crowd than the one that had come to hear Maya Angelou two months earlier," notes *Time*.[2]

The bustle reflects a general rightward shift in college students' views. Back in 1995, reports UCLA's Higher Education Research Institute, 66 percent of freshmen felt that the wealthy should pay a fatter chunk of taxes. Today, only 50 percent do. Some 17 percent of students now think it's important to take part in an environmental program, half the percentage that did in 1992. Support for abortion stood at two-thirds of students in the early 1990s; now it's just over half. A late-2003 Harvard University's Institute of Politics study found that college kids had moved to the right of the general population, with 31 percent identifying themselves as Republican, 27 percent as Democrats, and the rest independent or unaffiliated. "College campuses aren't a hotbed of liberalism anymore," Dan Glickman, director of the Institute of Politics, commented about the findings of the survey. "It's a different world."[3]

Youthful attitudes are volatile, of course, but this rightward trend may intensify. In a mock election run by Channel One, which broadcasts in public schools, 1.4 million high school students reelected George W. Bush in a landslide, with 55 percent of the popular vote and 393 electoral votes—greater than the 51 percent of the popular vote and 286 electoral votes he actually won.

These right-leaning kids sure don't look much like the Bill Buckley-style young Republicans of yesteryear. "There's been a big movement away from the stereotypical campus conservative," says Sarah Longwell, public-affairs director for the Intercollegiate Studies Institute (ISI). "Conservative students today will be wearing the same T-shirts, sneakers, and jeans that you find on most nineteen-year-old college kids."[4]

The new-millennium campus conservative is comfortably at home in popular culture, as I've found interviewing fifty or so from across the country. A favorite television show, for instance, is *South Park*. "Not only is it hilariously uncouth, but it also criticizes the hypocrisy of liberals," explains Washington University economics major Matt Arnold. "The funniest part is that most liberals watch the show, but are so stupid that they're unaware they're being made fun of," he says uncharitably. The young conservatives, again like typical college kids, also play their iPods night and day, listening less to Bach and Beethoven than to alt-rock, country, and hip-hop.

Yet the opinions of these kids are about as far from the *New York Times* as one gets. Affirmative action particularly exasperates them. Chris Pizzo, a Boston College political science major editing BC's conservative paper, the *Observer*, points to wealthy Cuban American friends from his native Florida, "raised with at least the same advantages and in the same environment that I was," yet far likelier to get into the top schools thanks to their ethnicity. Where's the justice in that? Pizzo asks. Worse still, many students argue, preferences carry the racist implication that blacks and Hispanics can't compete on pure merit, and in an open, dynamic democratic capitalist system like that in the United States, such condescension holds minorities back instead of helping them. "Affirmative action has a detrimental effect on the black community, whether or not we're willing to admit it," says Jana Hardy, a biracial recent graduate of Claremont McKenna College now working in urban planning.

The War on Terror, including the Iraq conflict, drew strong support from most of the students. Typical was Cornell classics major Sharon Ruth Stewart, mildly libertarian—except when it comes to fighting terror. "We have to use any and all means to defend ourselves from the terrorists, who hate the American way of life even more than the French and Germans do," she says. "That means bunker busters, covert ops, whatever ensures America is safe." University of Maryland junior Nathan Kennedy is just as tough-minded. "I am full-fledged on board with the Iraq War," he says. "We've brought the fight to the terrorists' door, dealing with the radical fundamentalist Arabs who want us all dead."

On cultural issues, the students had clearly reached their own, sometimes idiosyncratic, conclusions. Yale senior Nikki McArthur (a big Metallica fan) is, like most of the students I questioned, ardently pro-life—"but not because I necessarily think that an embryo is a full human being." Rather, she argues, "I think that a culture in which abortion is widely accepted is one in which people have a wrong understanding of children and sex. Children should not be considered burdens." Jordan Rodriquez, a rugged-looking evangelical Princeton undergrad, fraternity pledge president (Delta Kappa Epsilon), and hyperachiever—in high school in San Antonio, he was on the varsity baseball team, edited the school literary magazine, and played viola for the city's Youth Philharmonic—is the son of two centrist Republicans, but on abortion, he's as hard-line as they come. The practice is "ethically abominable," he says, and should be regarded as "a form of homicide and prosecuted as such."

Many of the students, especially the women, emphasized getting married and raising a family as primary goals in ways that would thrill the Family Research Council. "I'm an old-fashioned girl," avers Cornell's Stewart. "I think it's wonderful when a mother can spend the majority of her time devoted to her child's early years. I plan to do just that." University of Virginia sociology professor W. Bradford Wilcox, a recently minted Ph.D., has been seeing the same thing I have. "My biggest surprise in teaching here is that I am coming across growing numbers of post-feminist college women," he relates.[5] "These women tend to be very bright and—other things being equal—would normally gravitate to feminist academics." Instead, Wilcox notes, they're looking for "a sane path forward for the revival of courtship and family life." Polling data suggest such sentiments are increasingly widespread. A 2001 survey, for instance, found that 88 percent of male high school seniors and 93 percent of females thought it extremely or quite important to have a good marriage and family life.

Yet for most of the conservative students I interviewed, traditional values did not extend to homosexuality. Though few support gay marriage, fewer still wanted the U.S. Constitution amended to ban it, and most were okay with state-sanctioned civil unions for gays. "I don't buy the prevalent argument that recognizing gay unions would undermine the institution of marriage," says Vanderbilt University sophomore Anne Malinee, the strongly pro-life editor of the *Vanderbilt Torch*, the school's conservative monthly. "Of all the issues elected officials could be focusing on, why this?" Similarly, Bucknell University history and economics major Charles Mitchell, culturally conservative in many respects, isn't worried about gay marriage. "I believe that homosexuality is a sin, because that's what the Bible says, but I also believe that if two people of the same sex love each other and can get a priest to marry them, the propriety of that is none of the state's business."

ISI's Longwell polled conservative kids in 2003 and got results similar to mine. "While about 90 percent of the conservative students are now pro-life, there's not the same degree of opposition to gay marriage that you find among older conservatives," she says. "And an overwhelming majority says 'yes' to civil unions." In this, the right-of-center students reflect a growing acceptance among younger people as a whole for some form of legal recognition for homosexual unions. If cultural conservatives want to win the long-term argument over same-sex marriage, they've clearly got to do a better job persuading younger right-of-center types.

What accounts for the growing conservatism of college students? The new media explored in earlier chapters have surely played a significant role, giving younger people easy access to ideas and reporting and laughs they previously would have had to go hunting for. But why arc the ideas themselves catching on?

Osama bin Laden has something to do with it. After September 11, Americans haven't trusted the UN-loving Left to defend the nation with sufficient vigor and patriotism, and many collegians agree. As of late 2003, long after top liberals were declaring the Iraq War a quagmire, college students backed the war at higher levels than did the American population. Today's college students, notes Edward Morrissey, "Captain Ed" of the popular conservative blog Captain's Quarters, "grew up on . . . moral relativism and internationalism, constantly fed the line that there was no such thing as evil in the world, only misunderstandings." Suddenly, on September 11, this generation discovered "that there are enemies and they wanted to kill Americans in large numbers, and that a good portion of what they'd been taught was drizzly pap."[6]

Yet a deeper reason for the rightward shift, which began well before September 11, is the Left's broader intellectual and political failure, a failure that its feeble response to Islamofascist terror has only brought into sharp relief (thanks in part to being exposed by bloggers and other new information sources). American college kids have come of age in a post-Reagan era that witnessed both Communism's fall and the unchained U.S. economy's breathtaking productivity. They've seen what anyone willing to work hard—whatever their race or sex or creed—can achieve in such an opportunity-rich system. "I've always been the sort of person to motivate myself to succeed," says University of North Carolina–Chapel Hill journalism major Debra McCown. "Meanwhile, I've watched people who grew up in a similar background, some with way more financial resources than I ever had, fail for reasons that were no one's fault but their own." "I'm only twenty, so I don't remember segregation or the oppression of women—in fact, my mother had a very successful career since I was a kid," another student observed in an online discussion.[7] "I look around and don't see any discrimination against minorities or women." Nanny-statism, cries about the economic injustice and "structural" racism or sexism of American capitalism, anti-globalization protests: It all sounds like BS to many kids today.

The destructive effects of liberal "just-do-it" values on the family—divorce, dads and moms too busy "chasing dreams" to watch their kids grow up, permissive parenting sliding toward indifference—are equally evident to many young people, who have sometimes painfully felt those effects themselves or watched them rip up the homes of their friends. Rejecting the "lifestyle" choices of their elders, some turn to family values (at least in theory) with the enthusiasm of converts. Even their support of homosexual civil unions may find its source in the rejection of the world of fragmented human relations that liberalism has produced. "Heterosexuals have already done a decent job of cheapening marriage on their own," observes Vanderbilt's Malinee.

Conservative ideas take on even greater allure to students when the authorities say they're verboten. From pervasive campus political correctness—the unfree speech codes, obligatory diversity-sensitivity seminars, and school-sponsored performances of the *Vagina Monologues*—to the professoriate's near-uniform leftism, with faculty Democrats outnumbering Republicans by at least seven to one (at Williams, it's fifty-one Dems to zero Republicans), everything aims to implant the correct left-wing attitudes in student brains. If every adult around you says: "You *must* think this!" is it any wonder that some kids respond: "*No, I don't!*" and are starting to look elsewhere—to the forbidden Right—for answers? "There's a natural and healthy tendency among students to question the piety of their teachers," Penn history professor Alan Kors noted a few months back. "And for so long the pieties, dogmas, and a set of assumptions being taught on college campuses have been found on the far Left."[8] The irony isn't lost on Daniel Flynn, director of the Campus Leadership program of the Leadership Institute. "The intention of many in academe is to evangelize left-wing ideas, but in effect what they're doing is often the opposite: piquing interest in the other side," he says, laughing.

Katherine Ernst, a recent New York University grad, confirms the point. Like many students I queried, Ernst already leaned right when she arrived on campus. But the leftist propagandizing of her professors made her conservatism rock-solid. "One professor, right after September 11, gave a terrorist-sympathy speech that went, you know: 'Oil, oil, oil, they're poor, we take advantage of them, it's really complicated, blah, blah, blah'—it was something that I and many other students living in our financial-district dorm enjoyed," Ernst says sarcastically. "The worst professor I ever had, though, was for a course in administrative law," she recalls. "Every class—no exaggeration—included at least five references to 'Bush was selected.'" A final straw for Ernst came when "the for-real Communist professor" Bertell Ollman walked out of a class he was teaching "to take part in some stupid protest march." So there you have it, says Ernst: "You pay thousands and thousands and the prof takes off to carry a 'No Justice, No Peace' sign around Union Square Park. How could anybody exposed to this kind of stuff *not* become a raging right-winger?"

UNC's McCown would agree. At her school, she complains, the liberal profs tend to "ram their political views down students' throats." One incident particularly outraged her. "I watched as a classmate, required to attend class in his military uniform, sat there silently as the professor ranted about how every member of the U.S. military is a 'baby killer' who enjoys violence—because what could he possibly say to a teacher who pronounced such things, with him sitting there in uniform?" Bucknell University grad Tom Elliot (profiled in a 2003 *New York Times Magazine* article on "hipublicans") experienced "quite a bit" of hostility in the classroom.[9] "I was constantly singled out and made to look ridiculous—responsible for the right-wing ideas being lambasted by the professor that day," he observes. Jordana Starr of Tufts listens to her media and politics professor berate conservatives week after week: Bush's reelection is the "apocalypse," Bush is an evil draft dodger, ad nauseam.

The leftism that so angers these students includes the trendy hey-hey-ho-ho-Western-civ-has-got-to-go theories that inform college courses from coast to coast. "In too many classrooms," says former Reagan secretary of education and now talk-show host William Bennett, "radical professors teach their students that Western thought is suspect, that Enlightenment ideals are inherently oppressive, and that the basic principles of the American founding are not 'relevant' to our time."[10]

College course catalogues often read like satires. Want to study English lit at, say, Penn? Freshmen take introductory classes like "Secrecy and Sexuality in the Modern Novel," taught by—no joke—Heather

Love. In the course description, Dr. Love explains that "many of the books that we consider 'great literature'"—the obligatory postmodern scare quotes signaling the supposed absurdity of the idea of aesthetic quality—"are noted as much for what they don't say as for what they do." Deconstructing Herman Melville and other dead white males, Dr. Love promises to uncover "what, if anything, they are hiding" about homosexuality, pederasty, and incest. That's for first-year students. Later on, English majors get to explore "postcolonial literature" with Professor Cynthia Port, who relies on radical authors Edward Said and Frantz Fanon to "revise imperial narratives, challenge assumptions about identity and otherness, and scrutinize the politics of language." And then they can enroll in Dr. Love's upper-level course "Theories of Gender and Sexuality" to study "reproductive rights; pornography, 'sex work' [prostitution in human-speak], and free speech; . . . and trans-gender activism," among other themes that seem to have zilch to do with English lit.

How about learning some history at Brown? Start with History 1: "Europe from Rome to the Eighteenth Century," taught by Professor Amy Remensnyder. Sounds pretty straightforward—but read the course description and you discover that Professor Remensnyder plans to chart "the complex divisions" of various groups within European societies "according to gender, class, and ethnicity," the Holy Trinity of postmodern intellectuals. In Early American History, Professor Karl Jacoby tosses aside the founders and trains his multiculti eye on "the Indian settlement" of America and "the experiences of 'ordinary' peo-ple"—how they "conceived of themselves as male and female, slave and free, black, white, and Indian." One could go on and on, as many edu-cation critics have—and these are far from the craziest examples.

The upshot of this pervasive nonsense, Bennett argues, isn't educa-tion but confusion over the import of knowledge, the universality of the human experience, and the Truth, with a capital T, of ideals and principles—beliefs that once were at the heart of a liberal education. "In the end," he says, "the central problem is not that the majority of students are being indoctrinated (although some are) but that they graduate knowing almost nothing at all. Or worse still, they graduate thinking that they know everything."[11]

A student, conservative or otherwise, who doesn't buy into the West-is-the-worst line can "have an awful time of it," maintains Harvard junior Jordan Hylden—above all in the humanities. "It is quite difficult in fields like literature, anthropology, the social sciences, and even religion to even be informed," he complains. "It's like an ivory echo chamber, where only the 'right'—subversive, anti-Western—ideas get a hearing." Small wonder enrollments in such fields have plummeted. The percentage of undergraduate degrees in the humanities, nearly 21 percent in the mid-1960s, fell to 12 percent or so by the 1990s and has never climbed back.

Some conservative-minded students stuck in a left-wing echo chamber keep their real views to themselves and parrot the "correct" line, fearing that otherwise they'll get a low grade. One earnest Princeton freshman, for instance, had to write a paper on same-sex marriage, which he opposes, for a constitutional law course taught by a very liberal, pro–gay marriage professor. "I radically altered my position to make it more in line with what my professor's beliefs are on this topic and many others—and I know what those beliefs are because she insists on starting each class with a diatribe covering any number of current political issues, in addition to mocking Supreme Court Justices Scalia and Thomas consistently," he says. A 2003 survey by the Independent Women's Forum found that anywhere from one-quarter to one-third of students had felt forced to check "their intellectual and philosophical honesty at the door in order to get good grades."[12]

Such self-censorship may become rarer, thanks in large part to several national organizations that have worked to open the university to genuine diversity of thought and are now starting to see their efforts bear fruit, just as the new media have opened news and opinion formation to long-excluded ideas. The national outfits are helping to create the myriad right-of-center student clubs and groups and are sponsoring the talks that institutionalize the conservative presence on campus, giving students who hold conservative views the self-assurance to express them publicly. This also boosts the numbers of students willing to at least explore such views. "There is no coercion or imposition going on," Bucknell's Mitchell editorialized in the *Washington Times*. Rather, a demand for conservative ideas "is simply being met by, you might say, intellectual entrepreneurs."[13]

Perhaps most significant is Students for Academic Freedom (SAF), founded in 2003 and already boasting 130 campus chapters. The group's key initiative to date: a campaign for an Academic Bill of Rights. Universities adopting it, willingly or by legislative decree, agree not to deny tenure to teachers or fail to hire them solely because of their "retrograde" conservative politics, as is common practice today, and to ensure that teachers keep their classes from becoming left-wing propaganda sessions. "What I've set out to do is to try to restore the educational principles that were in place before the generation of 1960s leftists infiltrated the university and corrupted it by transforming it into an ideological platform," explains founder David Horowitz, editor of FrontPage.[14] Legislation enacting variations of the bill is on the move in nineteen states. In Colorado, state colleges have adopted a version of the bill "voluntarily" to prevent the legislature from imposing even tougher rules.

In lobbying for the Academic Bill of Rights, SAF publicizes horror stories that its chapters gather. They include:

> a Spanish instructor telling his class, "I wish George Bush were dead"

> a public policy prof informing a student who planned on
> attending a conservative conference in Washington, "Well,
> then, you'll probably fail my course"
> a law professor proclaiming, "We all know that the R in Repub-
> lican stands for racist"
> and a criminology teacher who asked students to explain on a
> test why George Bush is a war criminal, and then gave an F to
> a student whose answer argued that Saddam Hussein, not W.,
> was the real monster[15]

Horowitz says conservative kids have usually just accepted such left-wing classroom demagoguery. "They're conservative, and their disposition is to suffer: 'That's just the way colleges are,'" Horowitz says. "What I've done as an ex-radical is to encourage them to see the injustices done to them as injustices—and do something about it."

Needless to say, the university establishment is downright angry about SAF's campaign—all the more so because, jujitsu style, it turns the Left's own language of "diversity" and "rights" against it. The liberal American Association of University Professors, in textbook Orwellian fashion, declares the Academic Bill of Rights a "grave threat" to academic freedom. In Colorado, one educator reportedly resorted to thuggery to try to put a stop to a legislatively mandated academic-rights bill. "A student whose professor at a state school threw him out of class, saying, 'I don't want your right-wing views in my classroom,' testified at a legislative hearing that the bill would be a good idea, since it would curtail that kind of behavior," Horowitz recalls. "Once the student gets away from the microphone, the chairman of the philosophy department from the state university in question comes up, jams the kid in the chest with his finger, and says, "I have a Ph.D. from Harvard, and I will sue your *fucking* ass if this bill passes." A legislator, overhearing the threat from this anti-Socrates, noted, "That's exactly why we need this bill of rights."

The idea of *intellectual* diversity seems to be catching on even where the Academic Bill of Rights hasn't yet appeared. Consider Columbia University, embroiled in controversy throughout the fall of 2004 because—as the *New York Sun* uncovered—leftist professors there have promoted a militantly anti-Israel agenda, embracing venomous Arab propaganda, with students who disagree facing harassment and derision. In a November editorial responding to the controversy, the liberal *Columbia Daily Spectator*, the school's major undergraduate paper, called for greater political balance on the faculty. "By not having a conservative voice hawk its wares in the hue and cry of the academic marketplace, Columbia is failing its students," the paper argued. "It should be self-evident that a faculty that speaks with unanimity on some of the most divisive issues of the day is not fulfilling its duty."[16] The New York ACLU has joined the fray, siding with—no surprise here—the professors accused of intimidation.

Students for Academic Freedom helps college kids resist classroom demagoguery, but where can a student go to get an education that doesn't ignore or just denounce conservative ideas, but instead explores them sympathetically? Some students indeed look to the new conservative media to supplement their education. "Excluding one great economics professor, I learned more from listening to Rush Limbaugh every day than from all the NYU professors I've had," says Katherine Ernst, not really joking. Several students told me they read National Review Online and FrontPage daily as reality checks on their classes.

But if a student's lucky, he's got a prof like Princeton political scientist Robert P. George, a rare conservative who not only survives but also thrives in academia. George has clearly sparked passionate intellectual interest among students. "Professor George's stamp on our intellectual formation is unmistakable," confided one, "especially when it comes to taking seriously such notions as natural law"—the unfashionable belief, once central to Western thought, that a law exists that obligates us because of our nature, independently of all conventions and legislation. Students particularly admire George's approach to intellectual debate. "For our papers," says Duncan Sahner, the intensely serious editor in chief of the *Princeton Tory*, the campus's conservative magazine, "he stresses the need to engage in what he calls the 'strongest possible lines of counterargument'—straw-man parries, he says, only hurt conservatism." Moreover, Sahner adds, "his interactions with those who disagree with him are great examples of professional courtesy."

George has helped students expand their intellectual horizons beyond liberalism not only by his teaching but through his four-year-old James Madison Program in American Ideals and Institutions, whose success is reflected in its tenfold increase in operating budget, to $1.5 million, since 2000. The program is a model of liberal education in the worthy, old-fashioned sense, running, among numerous activities, high-level lectures by conservative thinkers such as Supreme Court Justice Antonin Scalia and Harvard political theorist Harvey Mansfield, as well as talks by notable liberal scholars such as Arthur Schlesinger Jr. and Michael Sandel. As many as two hundred students come to some of the events. The program also enables George to appoint six or seven visiting Madison fellows, whose ranks have included such conservative lights as political scientists Angelo Codevilla and Hadley Arkes. "All of a sudden," says one Princeton faculty member, "you've got a critical mass of conservative adults on campus, and conservative views become live options for students." And Princeton's right-leaning students have formed a kind of community around the Madison Program, as I discovered when, on short notice on a crisp early November 2004 day, George gathered twenty-five or so of them to speak with me in front of a roaring fireplace at the school's Bobst Hall.

Since few schools—and even fewer elite schools—boast such profs and programs, other national groups have rushed in to supply some of what's missing. The Virginia-based Young America's Foundation (YAF), for example, sponsors over two hundred university lectures a year by leading conservatives such as *Weekly Standard* editor Fred Barnes and Christina Hoff Sommers, a critic of militant feminism. Every year, thousands of students attend YAF's conferences on the principles of a free society, some held at the Reagan Ranch in Santa Barbara, California, which the group bought in 1998. Other right-of-center groups—including the Independent Women's Forum, the Leadership Institute, and the Institute for Human Studies—also organize lectures and seminars for students.

The Intercollegiate Studies Institute (ISI), founded in 1953 but reinvigorated in recent years, plays perhaps the biggest role of all fighting the Left's campus domination. It sponsors hundreds of conservative campus talks and seminars a year, rooted in "the enduring Western intellectual patrimony" of political and economic liberty, limited government, the rule of law, moral truth, and personal responsibility. ISI's lectures are usually higher-brow than Young America's Foundation's: regular speakers include classicist Victor Davis Hanson and historian Forrest McDonald. Another key initiative from ISI, as we saw in the last chapter, is its series of "student guides," short books written by first-rate scholars that show undergraduates how to educate themselves in the classics of the Western tradition. In addition, ISI provides a comprehensive guide to colleges that, among other features, warns college applicants about the schools that are particularly PC and shows them how to find teachers committed to traditional scholarship, and it offers fellowships to conservative-minded students worth as much as $40,000. ISI has given students "an intellectual home beyond the parameters of the academy," says recent Harvard graduate Claire McCusker, now studying political philosophy in Paris.[17]

One of ISI's biggest boosts to campus conservatism has been to expand the number of right-leaning student publications. In the mid-1990s, ISI took over the remnants of Irving Kristol and William Simon's

Collegiate Network, a nonprofit that in the 1980s nurtured—both financially and intellectually—the creation of campus conservative publications (including the *Dartmouth Review* and the *Harvard Salient*) but that had since languished. Shelling out upward of $1 million a year on printing costs and journalistic training, ISI has the Collegiate Network humming. It now boasts eighty-five or so member publications at schools ranging from elite Columbia and the University of Chicago to small community colleges—a 50 percent jump from just a few years ago. More than eight hundred kids currently work on the papers. The Leadership Institute also helps start conservative student publications via start-up grants and its two-day Student Publication School, which teaches young journalists how to get school funding for conservative papers, sign up advertisers, and, more substantively, pursue stories. In 2004, it oversaw more than twenty start-ups.

At their best, these publications mix serious analysis of both national and campus issues with impertinent anti-liberal humor. The *Virginia Advocate* at the University of Virginia is a good example. A recent issue featured a thoughtful interview with conservative critic Paul Cantor on the highs and lows of popular culture as well as the latest installment of a satirical column written by "The Stinky Hippy" (a recurring olfactory complaint among right-of-center college kids). An autumn issue of the *Stanford Review* mock-reported rather leadenly on "The Penis Dialogues: *A journey of self-awakening . . . and penises*"—but also editorialized with sharp intelligence about "Musharraf's Deception" in the War on Terror.

The campus Left has greeted these publications with outrage. In 2003, at Roger Williams University in Rhode Island, to take one prominent example, the *Hawk's Right Eye*—judged by the College Republican National Committee to be the second-best conservative student paper in the country—published a spate of anti-PC articles until school officials said: "Enough!" University president Roy Nirschel blasted an

e-mail to the entire campus charging that the paper had "crossed seriously over the lines of propriety and respect," "flirted with racist and
anti-Islamic rhetoric," and—you guessed it—created a "hostile environment for our students and community." The school froze $2,700 in
campus funds granted to the paper. It was a "death blow" for the *Hawk's
Right Eye*, says editor Jason Mattera, that silenced it for the year.[18]

Student leftists, sometimes with the support of school officials, regularly try to shut down or shut up conservative student publications,
practicing "free speech for me but not for thee," as Nat Hentoff calls
it. In 2003, for instance, the liberal-controlled SUNY–Albany student
association, solely for political reasons, nixed student-activity funds for
the right-leaning *College Standard Magazine*. This, *Campus* reports,
came after the magazine had already faced months of harassment from
the campus Left, including disruptions of its meetings by radical
groups, thousands of copies stolen, and defacement of its display
stands with anti-conservative threats. The magazine's staff, claiming
discrimination against their conservative ideas, won a ten-month court
battle against the school to have their funding restored.

These student publications serve as ideal training grounds for future
right-of-center intellectual talent. "If you look at the conservative movement now, particularly among writers, it is filled with people who were
working on these papers," says the Leadership Institute's Daniel Flynn.
*Policy Review* editor Tod Lindberg and *New York Post* columnist John
Podhoretz, to take just two of many examples, both started out at the
*Chicago Criterion*, the University of Chicago's conservative student
paper. Like all student publications, the conservative papers teach students important skills, from how to make a deadline to writing for a
general audience, and can be a source of real friendship and community for the young journalists who work on them. "The alternative student paper serves as a kind of club for conservatives, giving them a
common activity, a unifying project, and that's proven very helpful over

the years," explains Harvard's Harvey Mansfield, an academic adviser for the *Harvard Salient*.[19]

Of course, conservative kids face the same social pressures that all students do. So how do conservative kids fare on the campus social scene? It varies by school. Students I interviewed who attended Southern schools said right-of-center kids were in the majority and set the campus tone outside of the classroom. Harris Martin, a history major at the University of Georgia, estimates that over 60 percent of UGA students tilt right. "The culture is a distinctly Southern conservative one—hunting, football, big trucks and SUVs, camouflage, old ball caps, fishing, country music, and Southern rock," he tells me. At Chapel Hill, observes undergraduate Debra McCown, "the fraternities on campus lean heavily Republican—they're likely to have Bush stickers on their cars, as well as the Bonnie Blue, Stars & Bars, palmetto tree, or other Southern symbols." At Clemson University in South Carolina, says poli-sci junior Andrew Davis, "the typical student is Republican," though most don't care much about politics.

The more politically correct culture prevailing at other schools, especially the Ivies, can be a problem for conservative students. Several first-year Princeton students, for instance, believed that being seen as a conservative would make it harder for them to be chosen for membership by one of the school's five prestigious "bicker" eating clubs—key sources of social standing on a status-conscious campus and *the* places to party. "I've avoided writing any major articles for the *Tory* because I'm afraid it could hurt me when it reaches the time for me to bicker," one freshman confessed. Two other students hesitated to talk with me for the same reason, while a third said that she too wouldn't write for the *Tory* until she had made it into a club.

But for all the anxiety of the Princeton students, conservative kids on most campuses are eager to engage their liberal classmates (at least the ones who aren't burning newspapers) and have sparked a genuinely two-sided conversation that so rarely occurs in the classroom. The University of Washington College Republicans, for example, hold regular debates with Young Democrats and other campus liberal groups. "I like to think we're talking to young people who may not have formed their views and convincing them our views are right," UW chapter head Nick Dayton recently observed.[20] At Cornell, says Sharon Stewart, the conservative kids have held friendly sporting events with liberal groups and even a "Pie the *Cornell Review*" contest, in which liberals could take their best shot—"both literally and in the debates the event sparked." The conversation can move right into the dorms. "My roommate and I used to spend hours watching old episodes of *The West Wing* on Bravo," says Yalie Nikki McArthur. "She is as liberal as I am conservative, and we always had little political debates during the commercial breaks."

Conservative students must also deal with the coed dorms and hookup sex, drink-till-you're-blitzed parties, and general chaos of campus life at many schools, vividly described by author Tom Wolfe in his 2004 novel *I Am Charlotte Simmons*. Liberal educators abetted and encouraged such behavior when they rejected any in loco parentis duties decades ago and began to celebrate the idea of college being a time of "experimentation" and "growth." For some libertarian kids on the right, the social scene is A-OK. "Say what you will about us," says University of Michigan junior Ruben Duren, "we like to party! More than our fair share of sex, alcohol, rock n' roll. Not so much drugs, though," he adds. He's a real South Park Republican, in Andrew Sullivan's sense. But for some conservative students, especially those from religious backgrounds, the bedlam can be unsettling.

Harvard's Jordan Hylden, a conservative Protestant, finds Wolfe's characterization of campus life "depressingly correct." As well he might, given the dean-supervised tailgate party for the Harvard-Yale football game in late autumn 2004, so out-of-control with drunkenness, drugs, and nudity that it made headlines in the *Boston Herald*. "Today's university is without morals or guiding principles, except one," Hylden contends: "to follow in all things the ideal of 'to thine own self be true'—individual desires, whatever they are, are affirmed, and the denial of these desires, by yourself or by another person or group, is the greatest possible evil."

Some conservative students feel considerable pressure to "grow." Jennifer Mickel, a Princeton sophomore majoring in Near Eastern Studies, is a Presbyterian from Monroe, Louisiana, and quite traditionalist in her moral values. She'll drink a bit, but random hook-ups are a big no. And she gets flak for it. "Many of my girlfriends describe their sexual exploits in graphic detail and tell me that I need to get over my 'penis fear,'" she confides. Many Princeton males, she says, expect sex, or at least "intimate preludes to it," to follow a conversation and a dance—and certainly a bite to eat—as naturally as night follows day. "I just don't understand how both boys and girls alike can throw around intimate acts so lightly," Mickel laments. Things are different back in Monroe, where the rules of courtship still apply (a point made to me about their hometowns by several Southern students). "It is such a pleasure to go home and have guys treat me like a lady. There is much less of a 'sexpectation.'" Lots of students, she says, do eventually get into serious, almost-married relationships at Princeton, but these often grow out of "repeated hook-ups." "Perhaps, in a way, it's like a new kind of dating," Mickel reflects wryly.

"Binge drinking and hook-ups are pretty pervasive in collegiate culture," says Vanderbilt's Anne Malinee. "Generally, students across the political spectrum, even self-confessed conservatives, participate to some extent." Recent Indiana University graduate (and now law student) Joshua Claybourn agrees: "It's not uncommon for me to hear, even among conservatives, something like this: 'I don't have time for a relationship, so of course I hook up,'" he reports. "And I can count on one hand, among the thousands of students I've met, those that refrain from drinking regularly."

Helping students resist such pressures are a growing number of vigorous student religious groups, preaching moderation. College campuses nationwide have seen a "religious upsurge" over the last decade, the *Christian Science Monitor* reports.[21] The Massachusetts Institute of Technology, for example, is now home to fifteen Christian fellowship groups, "a pretty stunning development for a university...where efficiency and rationality are embedded in the DNA of the cold granite campus," notes the *Boston Globe*, making the typical liberal assumption that one can't be both rational and an evangelical Christian.[22] A new UCLA survey found that three-fourths of college juniors say that religious or spiritual beliefs have helped develop their identities, and 77 percent say they pray.

The upperclassman leaders of these religious groups can set examples for younger students, as Princeton senior Renee Gardner, leader of Crossroads Christian Fellowship, tries to do with student drinking. "There's certainly pressure on most students involved in the typical social scene to drink to excess," says Gardner, who belongs to one of the top Princeton eating clubs, showing that the younger students might be overstating their worries about conservative values keeping them from becoming members. "I've chosen—as have many Christian friends—to abstain from drinking in those contexts, not only to make it simpler for us to avoid blurring the line between acceptable and unacceptable levels of drinking, but also to make others feel more comfortable who might not want to drink."

Conservatives still have a long, long way to go before they can proclaim the Left's control over the campus broken—even to the degree that liberals' comparable monopoly over the media of opinion and information has been broken. The professoriate remains a way-left-wing body, more likely to assign Barbara Ehrenreich than Milton Friedman,

Michel Foucault than Michael Oakeshott, and nothing, not even David Horowitz's indefatigable activism, is going to change that soon.

Nevertheless, thanks to enterprising students, groups like ISI and SAF, and the new information sources that have been the subject of *South Park Conservatives*, the Left's iron hold on academe is beginning to loosen. Anyone who cares about the education of our children—and the future politics of our country—can only applaud.

# Conclusion

So where are we now? On the Left, some say that *conservatives* now dominate the institutions of opinion and information—and that's a problem for the country. "The Right is winning the culture wars," bluntly asserted Slate's Timothy Noah, a thoughtful liberal, shortly after the cancellation of *The Reagans*. "Within the cultural sphere," he continued, "liberalism has been in retreat for a good quarter-century." In his view, liberalism's cultural "defeat" occurred sometime between 1985, when *Rambo II* refought the Vietnam War, and the early 1990s, when Rush Limbaugh's *The Way Things Ought to Be* "hijacked the *New York Times* bestseller list." No one, Noah concluded, can plausibly claim that liberals continue to exert greater influence than conservatives over the culture.[1] As for news sources, other liberal writers—Eric Alterman and conservative-turned-lefty David Brock—say that it's the Left that should be complaining about bias, not the Right.[2]

But hang on. While the Right, broadly construed, may no longer be losing the culture wars, it certainly hasn't won yet, and it's too soon to tell if it is winning. The changes that this book describes are brand-new, and liberals still control all the mainstream media outlets, from the networks to CNN to the *New York Times* and most other metropolitan dailies (to say nothing of the universities, where, as we've just seen, conservatives are only beginning to make inroads).

Yet the trends are moving the Right's way.

> Sure, FOX News has fewer viewers for a typical hour than do the network broadcasts. But its audience share is steadily growing, while the networks' share is shrinking. And unlike the networks, FOX is broadcasting news all day. Since the same viewers aren't watching Linda Vester in the afternoon and Hannity and Colmes at night, FOX's total daily viewership probably comes closer to or surpasses that of any one nightly news program. That would comport with the Pew Research finding that more than a quarter of American adults get news from FOX.

> The influence of blogs, both right and left, is growing exponentially. News outlets will need to rein in their biases or risk blogosphere exposure and ridicule—a lesson the *New York Times* and CBS News should have learned by now. The number of Americans getting their news from the Internet and other new-media alternatives will continue to increase. The free market in information is here.

> South Park conservatism (or anti-liberalism) will become more prevalent in popular culture and on the campus. The political correctness that this brash sensibility skewers is anathema to younger Americans. The Left will have to abandon its PC illiberalism or continue to lose ground politically and culturally. The biggest changes still to come will be in academe.

The transformations in media and culture that I've described already show that the liberal old guard has come to the end of this particular road. "Hypocrisy and aristocratic smugness are drawing the ancient regime to its death," observes Victor Davis Hanson. "Rather's now-ossified generation came of age in the heady Vietnam era, on the apparent premise that Main Street, USA, and the Kiwanis had given us Vietnam, Watergate, racism, and other isms and phobias—and that only hip, swashbuckling 1960s types could tell the American people the 'truth' about what the 'establishment' was up to."[3]

If there's one thing that unites FOX News, the blogosphere, conservative talk radio, and *South Park*, it's a rejection of such liberal elitism. That's a key reason the new conservative media does so well in attracting a younger demographic. If people tend to get more conservative as they get older, have kids, and start making some money, it's doubtful many young FOX or NRO enthusiasts are going to become left-liberals when they hit forty.

Over time, a greater number of right-of-center voices will find audiences, whether it's via talk radio, blogs, cable news, the press, the entertainment world, and even academe. The Left will have to re-examine, argue, and refine its positions, so many of which have proved disastrously wrong, and stop living off the past. It's hard to imagine that this development won't result in a broader, richer, deeper national debate—something liberals of an older, John Stuart Mill–stripe would have welcomed.

It's also likely to result in a more conservative America.

# Acknowledgments

**T**he idea for this book originated in a much-discussed autumn 2003 cover article for *City Journal* titled "We're Not Losing the Culture Wars Anymore," commissioned by my friend and colleague (and boss) Myron Magnet, *CJ*'s esteemed editor. Working with Myron is a joy, and endlessly illuminating too; not an issue goes by where he doesn't astound me with an insight, an argument, or a perfect solution to an editing problem. I owe him an enormous debt of gratitude. Whatever is of worth in this book bears Myron's imprint. He read the manuscript and made many helpful suggestions, and allowed me to draw freely on my published *City Journal* work (parts of Chapter Two, and much of Chapter Eight, have been adapted from material that appeared first in *CJ*). He's not responsible for whatever faults the book exhibits, needless to say.

My thanks go out to Larry Mone, president of the Manhattan Institute, as well, and David DesRosiers, the institute's executive vice president, who've helped make MI a place of cutting-edge social-policy thinking and intellectual debate, and to my *City Journal* compatriots, above all Ed Craig, Steve Malanga, and Jay Rufino, for their friendship and commitment.

*South Park Conservatives* is based on lots of interviews, and I'd like to extend my appreciation to all the following for taking time out of often busy schedules to answer my questions: David Asman, Michael Barone, Jeremy Beer, Tom Bevan, Joshua Claybourn, Peter Collier, Nick Di Paolo, Jed Donahue, Ed Driscoll, Dinesh D'Souza, Dennis Dutton, Daniel Flynn, Robert P. George, Norman Geras, John Gibson, Jonah Goldberg, Julia Gorin, Tim Graham, Sean Hannity, Michael Harrison, John Hawkins, Tom Hazlett, Nat Hentoff, David Horowitz, Kay Hymowitz, Stefan Kanfer, Mickey Kaus, Roger Kimball, Sarah Longwell, Kathryn Lopez, Daniel J. Mahoney, Bernadette Malone, Harvey Mansfield, Megan McArdle, John McIntyre, Brad Miner, Dick Morris, Chris Muir, Paul Musgrave, Jeffrey O. Nelson, Michael Novak, Erin O'Connor, Scott Ott, Virginia Postrel, Colin Quinn, Glenn Reynolds, Steve Ross, Christopher Ruddy, Harry Stein, Andrew Sullivan, James Taranto, Eve Tushnet, Eugene Volokh, Matt Welch, and W. Bradford Wilcox. (For anyone I've forgotten to mention, my deepest apologies.)

I'd like especially to thank Michael Novak and Harry Stein, who saved me from some errors and offered strong encouragement, and Sarah Longwell of ISI and Robby George and Bradford Wilson of Princeton, who arranged for me to interview many smart, engaged students—too many students to acknowledge here, but whose voices dominate my final chapter. At FOX News, Irene Briganti was exceedingly helpful in arranging interviews. Thanks too to Nick Schulz, editor of Tech Central Station, for allowing me to adapt several graphs from an article I wrote for that excellent webzine in my conclusion here.

I'm grateful to Regnery's Marji Ross and Harry Crocker for showing such enthusiasm for my book, and to Miriam Moore for her gentle prodding and fine editing. Paula Decker provided expert copyediting. My agent, Andrew Stuart, is a whirlwind of entrepreneurial and intellectual activity.

I'd like to thank my parents, Charles and Theresa Anderson, for their love and support. My two little boys, Luke and Nick, made finishing the book as difficult as possible, and I love them dearly for it—they're the best sons a dad could imagine.

And to my amazing wife, Amy, I dedicate this book. She knows why.

# Notes

## Introduction: A New Era

1. Les Moonves quoted on www.drudgereport.com, November 4, 2003.
2. On the chronology of Rathergate and the Klein quotes, see Jonathan V. Last's exhaustive account "What Blogs Have Wrought," *Weekly Standard*, September 27, 2004. See also Chris Weinkopf, "Rather's Ruin," *American Enterprise*, December 2004, where Reynold's quote appears. See also www.ratherbiased.com.
3. Lev Grossman, "Blogs Have Their Day," *Time*, December 27, 2004, 109.
4. Tom Brokaw quoted by Howard Kurtz, "Dan Rather, in the Eye of the Storm," *Washington Post*, October 3, 2004.
5. Mike Siegel, quoted by NewsMax, "'Power Talk!'—How the Information Revolution Defeated John Kerry," November 14, 2004.
6. Michael Barone, "Old News Industry Loses," *New York Sun*, November 15, 2004.
7. Andrew Sullivan, "South Park Republicans are the Future," *Sunday Times*, December 21, 2003. Stephen W. Stanton, "South Park Republicans," www.techcentralstation.com, October 7, 2002, and "Do South Park Republicans Exist?," www.techcentralstation.com, December 5, 2003.

## Chapter One: The Old Media Regime

1. L. Brent Bozell III, *Weapons of Mass Distortion: The Coming Meltdown of the Liberal Media* (New York: Crown Forum, 2004), 20–21.
2. For Rather and Jennings quotes, and other biased comments by media representatives in this chapter, where not otherwise indicated, see the Media Research Center's information-packed website, www.mediaresearch.org.
3. Brit Hume quoted by Scott Collins, *Crazy Like a FOX: The Inside Story of How Fox News Beat CNN* (New York: Portfolio, 2004), 86.

4. S. Robert Lichter, Stanley Rothman, and Linda Lichter, *The Media Elite: America's New Powerbrokers* (New York: Adler Publishing, 1986).

5. Lionel Trilling, *Beyond Culture: Essays on Literature and Learning* (New York: Viking Press, 1965), ix–xx. See also Michael Novak, *The Catholic Ethic and the Spirit of Capitalism* (New York: Free Press, 1993), 195–220.

6. Stanley Rothman and Amy E. Black, "Media and Business Elites: Still in Conflict," *The Public Interest*, Spring 2001.

7. Hassett and Lott's study, "Is Newspaper Coverage of Economic Events Politically Biased?," is available at http://ssm.com/abstract=588453. The authors summarize their findings in "Queasy About the Economy? May Be Headlines You Read," *Investor's Business Daily*, October 8, 2004.

8. Bernard Goldberg, *Bias: A CBS Insider Exposes How the Media Distort the News* (New York: Perennial, 2003), 69.

9. Dan Seligman, "Reality Check," *Commentary*, March 2002.

10. Bozell, 79.

11. Jean-François Revel, *The Flight from Truth: The Reign of Deceit in the Age of Information*, translated by Curtis Cate (New York: Random House, 1991), 238.

12. Dinesh D'Souza, *Letters to a Young Conservative* (New York: Basic Books, 2002), 120.

13. R. W. Apple Jr., "A Military Quagmire Remembered: Afghanistan as Vietnam," *New York Times*, October 31, 2001.

14. On recent war reporting, see Karina Rollins's thorough roundup: "Doubt and Derision over Baghdad," *American Enterprise*, July/August 2003. Also useful is Dick Morris, *Off With Their Heads: Traitors, Crooks & Obstructionists in American Politics, Media and Business* (New York: ReganBooks, 2003), 3–66.

15. John Hinderaker, "How the Associated Press Operates," www.powerlineblog.com, September 26, 2004.

16. Tim Graham, "Amazing Loss: The media threw everything, including the sink, at Bush," www.nationalreview.com, November 4, 2004.

17. Mark Halperin's memo quoted on www.drudgereport.com, October 8, 2004.

18. Laura Ingraham quoted by Peter Johnson, "Are the Media Playing Politics?" *USA Today*, October 11, 2004.

19. John Podhoretz, "Smoking Gun—ABC's ABC of Media Bias," *New York Post*, October 12, 2004.

20. Unity convention participants quoted in "Reporters cheer Kerry, but snicker for Bush," www.worldnetdaily.com, August 9, 2004.

21. On the media coverage of Kerry and Bush, see the Center for Media and Public Affairs website, www.cmpa.com. Quoting Evan Thomas is Diana West, "The Media for Kerry," *Washington Times*, October 22, 2004. Thomas had previously said that media bias could give Kerry an extra fifteen points.

22. Jon Friedman, "The Passion that Burned for Bush," www.cbs.marketwatch.com, November 5, 2004.

23. S. Robert Lichter, Linda S. Lichter, and Stanley Rothman, *Prime Time: How TV Portrays American Culture* (Washington, D.C.: Regnery, 1994), 79–178, 210–11, 274–300.

24. Kurtz and O'Donnell quoted on www.andrewsullivan.com, May 27, 2003.

## Chapter Two: Illiberal Liberalism

1. Douglass's observation comes from his 1857 speech "The Significance of Emancipation in the West Indies," which you can find in *The Frederick Douglass Papers* (New Haven: Yale University Press, 1986).

2. *Federalist Papers* 1 (New York: Barnes & Noble Books, 1996), 89.

3. Gore quoted by Jeff Jacoby, "Poisonous Rhetoric from a Would-Be President," *Boston Globe*, July 23, 1998.

4. Stuart Taylor, Jr., "Who's Exploiting Racial Divisions Now," *National Journal*, December 4, 1999, 3445.

5. Kerry quoted by Patrick Healy and Rick Klein, "Kerry Team, DNC Hit Bush on Guard Issue," *Boston Globe*, September 10, 2004.

6. Bond quoted by Bloomberg News, "Bush Declines N.A.A.C.P. Invitation," *New York Times*, July 10, 2004.

7. For Edley's outrageous characterization of the Thernstroms' book, see Jason Zengerle, "The Gatekeeper: Clinton and Gore's mentor on race," *New Republic*, March 22, 1999.

8. Rangel quoted by Richard Cohen, "Still Divided By Race," *Washington Post*, November 1, 1994.

9. Magnet responded to Wolf's charge: "Naomi Cries Wolf Over 'Racism,'" *Wall Street Journal*, November 16, 1999.

10. Interview with author.

11. Clinton quoted in Paul Bedard, "Radical Reforms Feel Clinton Wrath," *Washington Times*, February 25, 1995.

12. See Jeff Jacoby, "How the Right is Demonized," *Boston Globe*, December 21, 1995.

13. Owens quoted in Michele Parente, "Promoters of GOP Pact 'Worse than Hitler,'" *Newsday*, February 19, 1995.

14. Hadley Arkes, "Fear and Loathing in L.A.," *Wall Street Journal*, November 20, 1998.

15. Jonathan Alter, "Trickle-Down Hate," *Newsweek*, October 26, 1998.

16. Melanie Phillips, "Newspeak: the words you need to survive the future," *Sunday Times*, December 26, 1999.

17. Schroeder quoted by David Boaz, "Too Nice for Talk Radio?" *Atlanta Inquirer*, October 4, 2003.

18. Richard Cohen, "When Morality Begets Violence," *Washington Post*, January 23, 1997.

19. John Leo, "Avoid 'Climate' Control," *U.S. News & World Report*, November 9, 1998.

20. Interview with author.

21. Nat Hentoff, "Censorship at Cornell: No violation to burn student papers," *Washington Times*, June 26, 2000.

22. Herbert Marcuse, "Repressive Tolerance," in Robert P. Wolff, ed., *A Critique of Pure Tolerance* (Boston: Beacon Press, 1969), 109.

23. John Rawls, *Political Liberalism* (New York: Columbia University Press, 1993).

24. Berkowitz's insightful essay deserves a full reading: "The Debating Society," *New Republic*, November 25, 1996.

25. Robert H. Bork, "Our Judicial Oligarchy," *First Things*, November 1996.

26. For Scalia's brilliant dissents in *Romer* and other key cases, see Kevin A. Ring, ed., *Scalia Dissents: Writings of the Supreme Court's Wittiest, Most Outspoken Justice* (Washington, D.C., Regnery, 2004).

27. Interview with author.

28. Begala quoted in the *Weekly Standard*'s "Scrapbook," November 27, 2000.

29. Lieberman quoted by Dan Eggen and Helen Dewar, "Ashcroft Wins Nomination," *Washington Post*, February 2, 2001.

30. Charles Krauthammer, "Disqualified by His Religion?" *Washington Post*, January 19, 2001.

31. David Horowitz, "Democrats, with help from media, have waged an all-out war on Bush," *Philadelphia Inquirer*, October 12, 2004.

32. Morton Kondrake, "Despite New Charges, Democrats Still Lead in Low-Blow Department," *Roll Call*, September 30, 2004.

33. John Podhoretz, "Down 'n Dirty—Kerry Goes All Negative," *New York Post*, October 19, 2004.

34. Garry Wills, "The Day the Enlightenment Went Out," *New York Times*, November 4, 2004.

35. Jane Smiley, "Why Americans Hate Democrats—A Dialogue," www.slate.msn.com, November 4, 2004.

36. Richard J. Ellis, *The Dark Side of the Left: Illiberal Egalitarianism in America* (Kansas: University Press of Kansas, 1998).

37. Interview with author.

38. Camille Paglia, "Crying Wolf," www.salon.com, February 7, 2001.

## Chapter Three: Fighting Back: Conservative Talk Radio

1. William G. Mayer, "Why Talk Radio Is Conservative," *The Public Interest*, Summer 2004.

2. Ruder quoted by Thomas W. Hazlett and David W. Sosa, "Chilling the Internet? Lessons from FCC Regulation of Radio Broadcasting," available at www.manhattan-institute.org/hazlett/rahzl98.pdf.

3. John Corry, "Fairness Most Foul," *American Spectator*, November 1993.

4. Shirley quoted by Stephen Goode, "Earning Airtime for Conservative Ideas," *Insight on the News*, September 30, 2002.

5. Fein quoted by Ted Hearn, "Reagan's Imprint," *Multichannel News*, June 14, 2004.

6. Peter Huber, *Law and Disorder in Cyberspace: Abolish the FCC and Let Common Law Rule the Telecosm* (Oxford: Oxford University Press, 1997), 147.

7. Hearn, "Reagan's Imprint."

8. Harrison quoted by Michael Rust, "Tuning to AMerica," *Insight on the News*, July 17, 1995.

9. Laura Ingraham, "'Live' with TAE," *American Enterprise*, July/August 2003.

10. Jason Zengerle offers a good overview of Rush's rise in "Talking Back: The coming rise of liberal talk radio," *New Republic*, February 16, 2004.

11. Limbaugh quoted in Terry Eastland, "Rush Limbaugh: Talking Back," *American Spectator*, September 1992.

12. Ibid.

13. "The Playboy Interview: Rush Limbaugh," *Playboy*, December 1993.

14. Bennett quoted by James Bowman, "The Leader of the Opposition: Meet Rush," www.nationalreview.com, August 1, 2003. The article originally appeared in 1993.

15. "The Playboy Interview: Rush Limbaugh."

16. Richard A. Viguerie and David Franke, *America's Right Turn: How Conservatives Used Alternative Media to Take Power* (Chicago: Bonus Books, 2004), 184.

17. Mansfield quoted in Scott Walter, "Limbaugh in the Ivory Tower," *American Enterprise*, March/April 1996.

18. Virginia I. Postrel, "Interview with the Vamp: Writer Camille Paglia," *Reason*, August 1995.

19. Gingrich quoted by Viguerie and Franke, 187.

20. See David Barker, *Rushed to Judgment: Talk Radio, Persuasion, and American Political Behavior* (New York: Columbia University Press, 2002).

21. Michael Barone, interview with author.

22. James Bowman, "The Leader of the Opposition," www.nationalreview.com, August 1, 2003.

23. Limbaugh quoted in Katy Bachman, www.mediaweek.com, August 11, 2003.

24. Savage quoted by Ira Simmons, "A Conservative Talk Radio Primer," www.chronwatch.com, May 15, 2003.

25. See the website for Bennett's show: www.bennettmornings.com.

26. Hennen quoted by Brian C. Mooney, "Interviews Show Bush Tuned In to Right-Wing Radio," *Boston Globe*, August 26, 2004.

27. Ingraham, "'Live' with TAE."

28. Cuomo quoted by Ralph Z. Hallow, "Cuomo: Bush started 'class warfare,'" *Washington Times*, January 8, 2003.

29. Hart quoted by Sam Howe Verhovek, "Out of Politics, But Still Talking, Radio Style," *New York Times*, March 13, 1995.

30. Mayer, "Why Talk Radio Is Conservative."

31. Cohen quoted by Sam Howe Verhovek, "The Media Business: Talk Radio Gets a Spirited New Voice from the Left," *New York Times*, May 9, 1994.

32. Jamieson interviewed on PBS's *Now*, February 13, 2004.

33. Don Feder, "Why Liberals Find Talk Radio So Threatening," *American Enterprise*, March/April 1996.

34. Jonah Goldberg, "Al Franken's Suicide Mission: Liberals can't do talk radio," www.nationalreview.com, Februay 21, 2003.

35. Interview with author.

36. Mayer, "Why Talk Radio Is Conservative."

37. Brudnoy quoted by Feder, "Why Liberals Find Talk Radio So Threatening."

38. Irving Kristol, "America's Exceptional Conservatism," in *Neoconservatism: The Autobiography of an Idea* (New York: Free Press, 1995), 383.

39. Hendrik Hertzberg, "Radio Daze," *New Yorker*, August 11, 2003.

40. Thom Hartmann, "Talking Back to Talk Radio—Fairness, Democracy, and Profits," www.commondreams.org, December 3, 2002.

41. Diana Owen, "Talk Radio's Price: A culture of complaint," *Christian Science Monitor*, November 16, 1998.

42. NBC reporter Bob Faw, quoted by Feder, "Why Liberals Find Talk Radio So Threatening."

43. Daschle quoted by Howard Kurtz, "Daschle's Rush to Judgment," *Washington Post*, November 23, 2002.

44. Clinton quoted by Feder, "Why Liberals Find Talk Radio So Threatening."

45. Rush Limbaugh, "It's an Attempt to Make Talk Radio PC," *Electronic Media*, September 27, 2003.

46. John Fund, "The Stop-Rush Campaign: Why do Republicans want to muzzle Limbaugh?" www.opinionjournal.com, September 12, 2003.

## Chapter Four: The FOX Effect

1. Rupert Murdoch, "The Publishing Revolution: A View from the Inside," unedited transcript of the 1989 Wriston Lecture at the Manhattan Institute.

2. Moody quoted by Marshall Sella, "The Red-State Network," *New York Times Magazine*, June 24, 2001.

3. Interview with author. All subsequent quotes from Asman drawn from interview.

4. Hume quoted by J. Michael Waller, "Fox Outraces the Old Dogs," *Insight on the News*, October 29, 2002.

5. Ken Auletta, "Vox Fox: How Roger Ailes and Fox News are changing cable news," *New Yorker*, May 26, 2003.

6. John Micklethwait and Adrian Wooldridge, *The Right Nation: Conservative Power in America* (New York: Penguin Books, 2004), 164.

7. Interview with author. All subsequent quotes from Gibson drawn from interview.
8. Smith quoted by Scott Collins, *Crazy Like a FOX: The Inside Story of How Fox News Beat CNN* (New York: Portfolio, 2004), 214.
9. Hume quoted by Sella, "The Red-State Network."
10. Interview with author. All subsequent quotes from Hannity drawn from interview.
11. Bill O'Reilly, *Who's Looking Out for You?* (New York: Broadway, 2003).
12. Micklethwait and Wooldridge, 162.
13. Interview with author. All subsequent quotes by Morris drawn from interview.
14. CNN producer quoted by Sella, "The Red-State Network."
15. Al Gore interviewed by Josh Benson, "Gore's TV War: He lobs salvo at FOX News," *New York Observer*, December 2, 2002.
16. Dean quoted by Charles Krauthammer, "The Delusional Dean," *Washington Post*, December 5, 2003.
17. John Carroll, "The Wolf in Reporter's Clothing: The Rise of Pseudo-Journalism in America," *Los Angeles Times*, May 6, 2004.
18. Tim Rutten, "The News: A nation divided," *Los Angeles Times*, July 7, 2004.
19. Tom Shales, "The Book Tour Blues," *Electronic Media*, October 21, 2002.
20. Cronkite makes this claim in the "documentary" *Outfoxed*.
21. Overholser quoted by Peter Johnson, "Brit Hume Honor Triggers Protest," *USA Today*, February 2, 2004.
22. Pingree quoted by Michael Grynbaum, *New York Sun*, July 20, 2004.
23. Gitlin quoted by Auletta, "Vox Fox."
24. Ibid.
25. Laura Berman, "News-Watching Becomes an Exercise in Ideology as TV Splits Viewers," *Detroit News*, July 29, 2003.
26. Parsons quoted by Lynn Smith, "Employee Defends Fox News at Screening," *Los Angeles Times*, August 7, 2004.
27. Interview with author.
28. See the program's website, www.pipa.org
29. See Stephen F. Hayes, *The Connection: How al Queda's Collaboration with Saddam Hussein Has Endangered America* (New York: HarperCollins, 2004).
30. Ann Coulter, "Crazy-Like-A-Fox Viewers," May 13, 2004, www.frontpagemag.com.
31. William Safire, "Sarin? What Sarin?" *New York Times*, May 19, 2004.
32. James Taranto, "Unfair and Unbalanced," www.opinionjournal.com, October 7, 2003.
33. The memos were first posted by blogger Wonkette at www.wonkette.com.
34. Moody quoted by Howard Kurtz, "Tilting at the Right, Leaning to the Left," *Washington Post*, July 11, 2004.
35. Moody quoted by Deborah D. McAdams, "Focusing on the World View at Fox," *Broadcasting & Cable*, January 17, 2000.
36. See Tim Groseclose and Jeff Milyo, "A Measure of Media Bias," September, 2003. Available at www.cbrss.Harvard.edu.

37. Friedman quoted by Belinda Hulin, "Information Overload? Media in the next decade," published on the website of the Public Relations Society of America, www.employee.prsa.org.

38. Scarborough quoted by George Gurley, "Joe Scarborough: As anti-O'Reilly, he's a gentle bear," New York Observer, April 28, 2003.

39. Christopher Hitchens's quote reproduced on www.andrewsullivan.com, May 19, 2004.

40. Hyman quoted by Wes Vernon, "Sinclair, the Next Fox, 'Fair and Balanced,'" www.newsmax.com, January 29, 2004.

41. Margot Habiby, "Sinclair to Preempt 'Nightline' on ABC Stations, Cites Politics," www.bloomberg.com, April 29, 2004.

42. Faber quoted by Lisa de Moraes, "Stations to Boycott 'Nightline's' List of the Fallen," Washington Post, April 30, 2004.

43. The Kerry aide made the comments on FOX News's Dayside with Linda Vester. See "Kerry Aide Threatens Sinclair Broadcasting?!?" www.newsmax.com, October 12, 2004.

44. Walker quoted by Lynn Smith, "TV That's the U of 'W,'" Los Angeles Times, August 24, 2004.

45. Burt quoted by Kelley Beaucar Vlahos, "New Channel Challenges MTV," www.foxnews.com, July 21, 2004.

46. Harvey Mansfield, "The Virtues of C-SPAN," American Enterprise, September/October 1997.

47. Frantzich quoted by Alan McConagha, "The Master of C-SPAN," Washington Times, December 12, 1994. See Frantzich's book, co-authored with John Sullivan, The C-SPAN Revolution (Oklahoma: The University of Oklahoma Press, 1996), and Richard A. Viguerie and David Franke, America's Right Turn: How Conservatives Used New and Alternative Media to Take Power (Chicago: Bonus Books, 2004).

48. Jonah Goldberg, "Good and Decent C-SPAN," www.nationalreview.com, March 30, 2004.

49. Lamb quoted by Curt Schleier, "C-SPAN's Leonine Brian Lamb," Investor's Business Daily, April 14, 2004.

50. Mansfield, "The Virtues of C-SPAN."

## Chapter Five: South Park Anti-Liberals

1. Stone quoted in an online interview with South Park Studios, www.southparkstudios.com. Trey Parker added: "We avoid extremes but we hate liberals more than conservatives, and we hate them."

2. Stone quoted by Rob Owen, "George W. as Ward Cleaver?," www.post-gazette.com, July 19, 2001.

3. South Park scripts, excerpts, and downloads are available at www.southparkstudios.com and www.twiztv.com. Most episodes are now available on DVD, and episodes broadcast several times a week on Comedy Central.

4. Parker and Stone quoted by Andrew Breitbart and Mark Ebner, *Hollywood Interrupted: Insanity Chic in Babylon—the Case Against Celebrity* (Hoboken, NJ: John Wiley & Sons, 2004), 272.

5. Parker quoted by Heather Havrilesky, "Puppet Masters," www.salon.com, October 12, 2004.

6. Quotes reproduced on www.indcjournal.com, October 12, 2004.

7. Parker quoted in "Matt and Trey Answer the Twenty Questions," on www.spscriptorium.com.

8. Peter L. Berger, *Redeeming Laughter: The Comic Dimension of Human Experience* (New York: Walter de Gruyter, 1997), 157–74.

9. Colin Quinn quoted in "Comics Launch Smart-Aleck Bombs," *New York Daily News*, March 30, 2003.

10. Tough Crowd routines transcribed from watching the show.

11. See Ada Calhoun, "The New Offensive Line," *New York*, April 5, 2004.

12. See Steven Devadanam, "Colinoscopy," *Houston Press*, June 3, 2004.

13. Interview with author. All subsequent quotes from Quinn drawn from interview.

14. Interview with author. All subsequent quotes from Di Paolo drawn from interview.

15. Gerald Nachman, *Seriously Funny: The Rebel Comedians of the 1950s and 1960s* (New York: Pantheon Books, 2003).

16. Joke quoted by Robert Hicks, "Nick Di Paolo Tells it Like it Is," *Tennessean*, January 30, 2004.

17. Transcribed from Nick Di Paolo's CD, *Born This Way*.

18. Calhoun, "The New Offensive Line."

19. Interview with author. All subsequent quotes and jokes by Gorin drawn from interview.

20. Dennis Miller, "'Live' with TAE," *American Enterprise*, October/November 2003.

21. Miller interviewed by Rebecca Winters, "10 Questions for Dennis Miller," *Time*, December 22, 2003. Miller's next observation also drawn from this interview.

22. Miller, "'Live' with TAE."

23. For a whole collection of Dennis Miller "rants and monologues," see the fan website www.igorn.com.

24. Caryn James, "They're Celebrities, and You're Not," *New York Times*, February 8, 2004.

25. Comic riffs chiefly compiled by a hostile Amy Reiter, www.salon.com, January 27, 2004. The riff on Hussein's thuggish sons quoted by Catherine Seipp, "Dr. D. & DM: Dennis Miller drives the Left nuts," www.nationalreview.com, May 12, 2004.

26. Robert Fulford, "Dennis Miller Says What Most of Us Think," *National Post*, April 24, 2004.

27. Miller interviewed by James Hirsen, "Dennis Miller: Why I Ascended to the Right," www.newsmax.com, February 5, 2004.

28. Brendan Bernhard, "Miller's Crossing," *LA Weekly*, March 5, 2004.

29. Interview with author.

30. Eric Spratling and Craig Albrecht, interviews with author.

31. Gavin McInnes, "Hip to Be Square: It's getting cooler to be conservative," *American Conservative*, August 11, 2003. After some observers claimed McInnes's article was written in jest, I queried him. "I stand by what I wrote in the *American Conservative*," he replied. "Some of the examples may have been exaggerated but the truth is, young people are sick of liberal naiveté."

## Chapter Six: The Blogosphere

1. Interview with author.

2. Interview with author.

3. Edward B. Driscoll, Jr., "Is the Blogosphere Half-Empty, or Half-Full?" www.techcentralstation.com, March 15, 2004.

4. Rod Dreher, "Welcome to the Blogosphere," *Dallas Morning News*, June 23, 2004.

5. Interview with author.

6. Interview with author.

7. Camille Paglia, "Drudge Match," Radar, Summer 2003.

8. See "The Secrets of Drudge Inc.," *Business 2.0*, April 2003.

9. Interview with author.

10. Barone, Cook, and Brooks quoted on www.realclearpolitics.com.

11. Dutton and Tran Huu Dung quoted by Scott Galupo, "A & L Daily: After famine, a feast of ideas online," *Washington Times*, January 25, 2003.

12. Interview with author. All subsequent quotes by Goldberg drawn from interview.

13. Interview with author.

14. Greenfield quoted by Paul J. Gough, "Convergence," www.hollywoodreporter.com, July 27, 2004.

15. Interview with author.

16. Interview with author.

17. Interview with author. All subsequent quotes by Kaus drawn from interview.

18. Interview with author.

19. Interview with author.

20. Dennis Miller, "'Live' with TAE," *American Enterprise*, October/November 2003.

21. Glenn Reynolds, "On the Warpath: Blogs are now so powerful that the media are catching up," *Guardian*, February 20, 2003.

22. See their fascinating working paper "The Power and Politics of Blogs," available at www.danieldrezner.com.

23. Interview with author.

24. Andrew Sullivan, "Lott's Rife," *New York Sun*, June 6, 2003.

25. Glenn Reynolds, www.instapundit.com, September 13, 2004.

26. Jeff Jarvis, "Dan's Mistake: what the old media need to learn from the new," *New York Post*, September 20, 2004.

27. Okrent quoted on www.andrewsullivan.com, October 5, 2003.

28. Keller quoted by Howard Kurtz, "Bill Keller's Changing Times," *Washington Post*, November 24, 2003.

29. Zeyad, "A Great Day for Iraq," www.healingiraq.com. December 10, 2003.

30. James S. Robbins, "Comparative Barbarism: What we learn from Nicholas Berg's murder," www.nationalreview.com, May 12, 2004.

31. Ali quoted by Cesar G. Soriano, "Iraqis Enjoy New Freedom of Expression on Web Journals," *USA Today*, April 20, 2004. Ali had shared the Iraq the Model blog with his brothers Mohammed and Omar, but launched his own site in late 2004.

32. Motallebi quoted by Mark Glaser, "Iranian Journalist Credits Blogs for Playing Key Role in His Escape from Prison," www.ojr.org, January 1, 2004.

33. See Daniel W. Drezner and Henry Farrell, "Web of Influence," *Foreign Policy*, November/December 2004.

34. Hugh Hewitt, "Rise of the Milblogs," www.weeklystandard.com, March 11, 2004. See Hewitt's book *Blog: Understanding the Information Reformation That's Changing Your World* (Nashville, TN: Thomas Nelson, Inc., 2005)—the first book on the blogosphere's coming influence not only in politics but in culture, business, and other fields. Hewitt is also a successful radio talk show host, as we pointed out in Chapter Three.

35. Glenn Harlan Reynolds, "The Blogs of War: How the Internet is reshaping foreign policy," *National Interest*, Spring 2004.

36. "LisaS," "What Liberal Media???" www.rightvoices.com, September 3, 2004.

37. Glenn Harlan Reynolds, "The Future of Blogs and the Blogosphere," www.techcentralstation.com, October 27, 2004.

38. Hugh Hewitt, "Trouble in South Dakota...for Tom Daschle," www.weeklystandard.com, July 8, 2004. See also John Fund, "How Daschle Got Blogged," www.opinionjournal.com, December 13, 2004. Fund, like Hewitt, is a keen student of new media.

39. Duff McDonald, "Taranto's Web," *New York*, September 6, 2004.

40. Interview with author.

41. Interview with author. A collection of Ott's best parodies has been published: Scott Ott, *Axis of Weasels* (Pennsylvania: MacMenamin Press, 2004).

42. Interview with author.

43. Alex Beam, "In the World of Web Logs, Talk is Cheap," *Boston Globe*, April 2, 2002.
44. David Broder, "The Media, Losing Their Way," *Washington Post*, September 26, 2004.
45. Randell Beck, "Web Log Junkies Welcome Here," *Argus Leader*, July 25, 2004.
46. Cass Sunstein, *Republic.com* (Princeton: Princeton University Press, 2001), 49. Quoted by Drezner and Farrell, "The Power and Politics of Blogs."
47. Jack Balkin, "What I Learned About Blogging in a Year," www.balkin.blogspot.com, January 23, 2004. Quoted by Drezner and Farrell, "The Power and Politics of Blogs."
48. Matt Welch, "Blogworld and its Gravity," *Columbia Journalism Review*, September/October 2003.
49. John Fund, "Beantown Becomes Blogtown," www.opinionjournal.com, July 26, 2004.

## Chapter Seven: The Conservative Book Publishing Revolution

1. Christopher Dreher, "Right Turn: Conservative publishing comes of age," *Publishers Weekly*, June 30, 2003.
2. Michael Novak, Jed Donahue, and Dick Morris, interviews with author.
3. Ross quoted by Patti Thorn, "America's Reading from Left to Right," *Rocky Mountain News*, July 12, 2003.
4. Peter Collier's comments are on the Encounter website, www.encounterbooks.com.
5. Interview with author.
6. Nelson quoted by Christopher Dreher, "Tide Rises for ISI Books," *Publishers Weekly*, July 21, 2003.
7. Interview with author.
8. Galvin quoted on the ENC website, www.encpress.com.
9. Wilhelm quoted by Nicole LaPorte, "Book Biz Turns Right," *Daily Variety*, May 21, 2003.
10. Interview with author. All subsequent quotes by Miner drawn from interview, except where noted.
11. Bellow quoted by Dreher, "Right Turn: Conservative publishing comes of age."
12. Interview with author.
13. Regan quoted by Dreher, "Right Turn: Conservative publishing comes of age."
14. Interview with author. All subsequent quotes by Ross drawn from interview.
15. Interview with author.
16. Bellow quoted by Dreher, "Right Turn: Conservative publishing comes of age."
17. Shirley interviewed by Stephen Goode, *Insight on the News*, September 30, 2002.
18. Interview with author.
19. O'Reilly quoted in "The New York Times Pravda Review," www.foxnews.com, November 17, 2003.
20. Gene Edward Veith, "Chain Reaction," *World Magazine*, June 7, 2003.

21. Interview with author.
22. See Jay Nordlinger's "Little Suppressors: Dealing with the bookstore clerk who hates you," *National Review*, September 27, 2004.
23. Vin Altruda, "Letters," *National Review*, October 25, 2004.
24. Interview with author.
25. Provizer quoted by Thorn, "America's Reading from Left to Right."
26. Ellen E. Heltzel, "Manhattan Takes a Right Turn," www.poynter.org, May 7, 2003.

## Chapter Eight: Campus Conservatives Rising

1. Interview with author. All student quotes drawn from author interviews, except where noted.
2. John Cloud, "The Right's New Wing," *Time*, August 30, 2004.
3. Glickman quoted by Alaina Sue Potrikus, "New Schools of Thought: College students have become more conservative than the general population, according to a new poll," Knight Ridder News Service, October 24, 2003.
4. Interview with author. All subsequent quotes by Longwell drawn from interview.
5. Interview with author.
6. "Captain Ed," "How the Left Lost Younger Voters," www.captainsquartersblog.com, May 4, 2004.
7. The observation responds to "How the Left Lost Younger Voters."
8. Alan Kors quoted by Mike Newall, "'We're the Antiestablishment Now,'" *Philadelphia Weekly*, August 25, 2004.
9. See John Colapinto, "Armies of the Right: the Young Hipublicans," *New York Times Magazine*, May 25, 2003.
10. See William J. Bennett, "Introduction" to *Choosing the Right College: The Whole Truth About America's Top Schools* (Grand Rapids, Michigan: William B. Eerdmans Publishing Company, 2001), xiii.
11. Ibid., xiv.
12. See "The Forgotten Generation: IWF Nationwide Survey of College Students," January 14, 2004, available on IWF's website, www.iwf.org.
13. Charles Mitchell, "The Conservative Mafia," *Washington Times*, October 19, 2003.
14. Interview with author. All subsequent quotes by Horowitz drawn from interview.
15. For these and other reports, see SAF's website, www.studentsforacademicfreedom.org.
16. Staff editorial, "A Call for Conservatism: several documents lack ideological diversity," November 9, 2004. Available at www.columbiaspectator.com.
17. Claire McCusker, "ISI: There at the Beginning," *Campus*, Fall/Winter 2003.
18. See Jason Mattera, "Roger Williams Witchhunt," October 21, 2003, www.frontpagemag.com.
19. Interview with author.

20. Dayton quoted by Marc Ramirez, "For Some, College Starting to Look Right," *Seattle Times*, October 29, 2004.
21. Amanda Paulson, "Religious Upsurge Brings Culture Clash to College Campuses," *Christian Science Monitor*, December 10, 2003.
22. Neil Swidey, "God on the Quad," *Boston Globe Magazine*, November 30, 2003.

## Conclusion

1. Timothy Noah, "The Right Declares Victory," www.slate.com, November 10, 2003.
2. See Eric Alterman, *What Liberal Media? The Truth About Bias in the News* (New York: Basic Books, 2003) and David Brock, *The Republican Noise Machine: Right-Wing Media and How it Corrupts Democracy* (New York: Crown, 2004).
3. Victor Davis Hanson, "The Fall: A bankrupt generation is fading away," www.nationalreview.com, September 24, 2004.

# Index

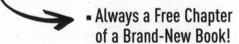